Going Over

A Nova Scotian Soldier in World War I

David Mossman

Pottersfield Press, Lawrencetown Beach, Nova Scotia, Canada

Library and Archives Canada Cataloguing in Publication

Going over : a Nova Scotian soldier in World War I / David Mossman.
Includes bibliographical references.
ISBN 978-1-897426-61-6 (pbk.)
1. Mossman, Titus, 1894-1974. 2. Soldiers--Nova Scotia--Biography.
3. Canada. Canadian Army. Battalion, 85th--Biography. 4. World War, 1914-1918--Personal narratives, Canadian. 5. World War, 1914-1918--Psychological aspects. 6. Soldiers--Family relationships--Nova Scotia.
I. Title.

Cover design by Gail LeBlanc
Cover image from the Mossman family

We acknowledge the financial support of the Government of Canada through the Canada Book Fund for our publishing activities. We acknowledge the support of the Canada Council for the Arts, which last year invested $157 million to bring the arts to Canadians throughout the country. Nous remercions le Conseil des arts du Canada de son soutien. L'an dernier, le Conseil a investi 157 millions de dollars pour mettre de l'art dans la vie des Canadiennes et des Canadiens de tout le pays. Pottersfield Press recognizes the support of the Province of Nova Scotia through Film and Creative Industries Nova Scotia. We are pleased to work in partnership with the agency to develop and promote our creative industries for the benefit of all Nova Scotians.

Pottersfield Press
83 Leslie Road
East Lawrencetown, Nova Scotia, Canada, B2Z 1P8
Website: www.PottersfieldPress.com
To order, phone 1-800-NIMBUS9 (1-800-646-2879) www.nimbus.ns.ca

The Canada Council for the Arts Le Conseil des Arts du Canada Canada FILM & CREATIVE INDUSTRIES NOVA SCOTIA

Contents

Prologue

There are several stories here and possibly several small books. But that's life, and in a manner of speaking, many of us have lived several lives.

My father, Titus Milton Mossman, was born in the late 1800s in Upper Kingsburg, Lunenburg County, Nova Scotia, a relatively isolated, religiously strict community shaped by Calvinist Presbyterianism. True to his "Bluenose" roots, he would earn his keep aboard Grand Banks schooners through his teenage years. Then, at his own initiative, he joined the Canadian Corps, becoming "222568 Rifleman Mossman" to ship overseas with a cross-section of Nova Scotia society, all packed into a troopship like livestock to fight in one of the world's most soul-destroying wars. In his final chapter as a family man, Titus the physically unscathed survivor would live into old age, alone with his post-traumatic nightmares, a stranger in many respects to his own family.

The book you hold tells the life and times of the early-twentieth-century Nova Scotia everyman and, more specifically, my father, in so far as I am able to reconstruct them. Many of the incidents and issues are as brief and authentic as the man himself. Fortunately, his youngest son is a compulsive diarist, and my closet is replete with dusty, roughly pencilled, and mostly unpublished records. Most of the conversations, unless otherwise indicated, are in the realm of historical fiction, created from my memory as close to real life as possible. The main characters are real; the minor characters are people well known to Titus. Events in his life while in the 85th Battalion, Nova Scotia Highlanders, unroll in order, following the War Diary of the 85th Nova Scotia Highland Regiment. That document was maintained on a daily basis by the Adjutant of the 85th Canadian Infantry Battalion and subject at each month's end to the approval of the Commanding Officer, Lt. Col. Allison H. Borden.

Time marches on. My appreciation of Father's sacrifice in response to military exigencies has been sharpened on several accounts. One is my very small part in a bush war in the former Central African Federation, far removed from mainstream remembrance and concern. But the prime mover in shaping this manuscript is the one hundredth anniversary of the start of the Great War (1914-1918), and a desire to record the profound effect the war had on Titus the man, and on his family. There is too his modest wartime archives contained in a small metal box, and several of the old soldier's maps and photographs, given in trust to me by my mother. I am keeping a promise to make use of these vestiges of a life lived at the sharp edge of history.

David Mossman
Wolfville, Nova Scotia
December 30, 2013

Three of the most senior "old originals" in the 85th Battalion relax at Rixensart, Belgium, following the armistice. On the right is Company Sergeant Major Titus M. Mossman, father of the author and the subject of this book. On the left is an unidentified sergeant. In the centre is Company Sergeant Major Howard H. Hastings of New Waterford, Cape Breton. Titus and Howard each wear a revolver and a canvas belt for holding a soldier's "small pack."

Timeline

September 1750 – Titus Mossman's ancestors arrive in Halifax, Nova Scotia on *Ann*, from Europe.

January 1, 1894 – Titus Milton Mossman is born.

1907 – Titus goes to sea as a flunkey on a Grand Banks schooner.

August 13, 1914 – Britain declares war.

September 24, 1915 – 85th Nova Scotia Highlanders Battalion is formed.

October 7, 1915 – Titus signs up with the 85th Battalion.

October 13, 1916 – The 85th departs Halifax for U.K. on R.M.S. *Olympic.*

October 19, 1916 – The 85th arrives in Liverpool, U.K.

February 10, 1917 – The 85th arrives in France.

April 9-14, 1917 – Battle of Vimy Ridge.

June 1917 – "The Triangle," Ontario Trench, Eleu dit Leauvette, Avion Horse Shoe.

June 20-28, 1917 – Titus's best friend Private William E. Harris of New Ross, Nova Scotia, is killed.

July-October 1917 – Lens.

August 29, 1917 – Titus begins a 10-day leave in Paris.

September 22 to December 11, 1917 Titus is in hospital, Étaples-sur-Mer, France.

October 28-November 2, 1917 – Passchendaele.

January 3 to July 31, 1918 – The long march to Amiens.

April 16-May 6, 1918 – Arleux.

July 24-31, 1918 – Fampoux.

August 8-11, 1918 – Amiens.

August 10, 1918 – Titus is awarded the Military Medal for his actions at Rosiéres-en-Santerre.

September 2-5, 1918 – Arras, Mont Dury, Drocourt-Quéant Line.

September 2, 1918 – Titus is awarded the Bar to the Military Medal.

September 27-October 1, 1918 – Cambrai (Bourlon Wood).

October 23-November 2, 1918 – Valenciennes, Mons.

November 1918 – Quievrechain.

November 1918 – Honnelle River.

November 11, 1918 – Armistice is declared.

May 1, 1919 – The 85th departs France for England.

May 3, 1919 – The 85th and Titus participate in the Great March of Triumph through London.

May 31, 1919 – Titus and the 85th sail from England on the *Adriatic* for Canada.

June 8, 1919 – *Adriatic* docks in Halifax; troops are welcomed home.

September 1919 – Titus returns to the sea.

September 20, 1928 – Titus marries Helen Viola Spindler.

September 1928 to August 1974 – Conflict continues on the home front.

August 19, 1974 – Titus passes on.

Introduction

(early winter, Rose Bay, 1948)

Imagine yourself in the kitchen of a fisherman's house in the village of Rose Bay on the South Shore of Lunenburg County, Nova Scotia, in the late 1940s. The home is that of my parents, Titus and Helen Mossman, Bluenosers both.

Mother is a well-educated schoolteacher. Father has little formal education and is home after his latest fishing trip, from what would prove to be a lifelong career as sea cook. A socially outgoing mother of three, Helen grew up in Rose Bay, and is proud of it. Titus, no less proud perhaps, but known more for his dour nature and unpredictable mood changes than for his social skills, is from Upper Kingsburg, a small village less than three miles by dirt road south of Rose Bay. During the Great War of 1914-1918, he advanced from private through the ranks of non-commissioned officers to Company Sergeant Major in the 85th Canadian Infantry Battalion, Nova Scotia Highlanders.

Their youngest child, I am a boy of eleven years, seated by the kitchen table doing homework. My older sister and brother are away at college. The time is five to five, on a weekday, minutes to dinner in this disciplined home. Outside, night is falling, scarcely distinguished now from late afternoon amidst the foggy drizzle of a day in early winter.

"God almighty, woman! Can't you stand watch for five minutes?" Titus roars, as he shoots out of his armchair by the kitchen window. Bounding into the centre of the room where a pall of bluish-grey smoke is beginning to swirl, he flails his arms wildly in an attempt to clear the air. In one swift motion he swings about, sweeping the pot of burning rice off to the side of the stove.

Emerging from her tiny pantry, Mother stands, hands on apron, momentarily stunned by the outburst. Trapped at the dinner table, I sit back, cringing fearfully in the face of this sudden domestic storm. It is hardly the first blow-up to occur in this household, but it seems no one ever quite gets used to it. That anyone ever will is of course rather unlikely; in every case the ending is uncertain.

"Can't you keep an eye on t'ings? You'll burn the bloody place down one of these times. Clumsy klotz! Can't you even cook rice?"

"Get a hold on yourself, Titus. It's not the end of the world. There's no need to shout. And for Heaven's sake, put your teeth in. You look a sight. And mind the child."

"Shut up, woman! I'll speak whenever I want!"

"Don't need to fly off the handle. Why are you so worked up? No wonder neighbours never drop by when you're home."

"What do you mean? I live here too. I know my job, an' my place, an' so should you, dammit!"

Abandoning defense, Helen poises for the counterattack. Well-practiced after more than twenty years of marriage, she delivers, squeezing off the hair trigger to her husband's hidden but heartfelt pride in position during that great and terrible first world war thirty years earlier.

"There you go again. Sure you sound just like some old company sergeant major. Ten'shun! Hup one two!"

"God damn it, woman, you're an aggravation!" Titus explodes in rage. "For all your fancy schoolin' you t'ink you know it all. What do you know about it anyway ... you can't even run your own kitchen."

"You're not on the parade square, Titus. Sit down, man, for Heaven's sake and try to control yourself."

"I'll sit down when I'm good an' ready. You'll not tell me what to do, an' when!"

In a crowning touch to her mockery, Mother raises the stakes in this standoff, chiding her husband of his upbringing.

"It's the same old tirade. Won't you ever grow up? But I suppose that's expecting too much for someone brought up in the back and beyond out in the woods of Upper Kingsburg!"

"What's that about Upper Kingsburg, hey?"

"Kingsbuggers! Bah!"

"Shut your yappin', woman, or I'll clout you one!"

Derision, impatience, annoyance, fear, even daring – the child recognizes all these flashing signals on display, tempting fate like a red flag as the bull turns.

The strong right arm rises quickly. But the threatened backhand delivery does not materialize. Seeing this, I try breathing normally again, praying for an end to the crisis.

Titus turns then and makes his way from the kitchen through the door leading into the cold unheated entry. Perhaps the worst is over and done with, for now. Behind him, the smoke in the kitchen thins. No clear winner certainly.

"Guess I'm not wanted around here. Might as well jump into the cesspool an' make an end of it," he mutters, passing through the door on his way outside. Through the kitchen window it is too dark and foggy now to see the top of that pillbox-like nine-foot-deep concrete structure buried in the ground and hunched beside the driveway. But the reality of its presence, like the old soldier's threat, remains all too palpable.

PART I

BACKGROUND

1

Setting the Scene

The story of the foreign Protestant migration to and settlement in Nova Scotia does not blaze with the stirring episodes or the brilliant human actors that make for historical high drama.

– The "Foreign Protestants" and The Settlement of Nova Scotia
Winthrop Bell

The story of my father's New World ancestry begins in Europe during the Reformation, that sixteenth-century split in Western Christianity. The conflict between Roman Catholics and Protestants continued through the eighteenth century, inciting concern about corruption in the church, war among princes, and uprisings among peasants. As refugees from this turmoil, Titus's forbears answered a 1750 British proclamation in Germany offering land and associated privileges in the colony of Nova Scotia.

Prospective settlers of Swiss, German and French origin amassed in the port of Rotterdam. In total, 1,615 farming folk were dispatched over a three-year interval to Halifax, Nova Scotia. They travelled across the Atlantic Ocean on ten small brigs known as "snows," the largest of all old two-masted vessels. People paid for their passage in Dutch currency, although most of them signed on as debtors under the relatively benevolent eye of John Dick, who was a well-connected Scottish businessman. Dick acted on behalf of the British government, in an effort to recruit loyal and industrious Protestants to help counterbalance the French presence in Nova Scotia.

On Monday, June 29, 1750, Titus's Swiss ancestors set sail from Rotterdam on the 230-ton *Ann*, carrying a complement of 322 people. According to available reports, rations during the voyage were rather sparse. Although Dick reportedly saw to it that *Ann* was victualled for a fourteen-week voyage, survivors told a different tale on their arrival in Halifax. Their blunt assessment was that they had been served up foul water and putrid, wormy, and totally inadequate food. All told, seventeen bodies were placed in stitched canvas shrouds, weighted with rocks, and dropped ceremoniously over the side during *Ann*'s three-month passage across the North Atlantic. For most of the immigrants on board, the voyage was an absolute nightmare.

Only a tiny amount of space had been allotted between decks for accommodation, and even that lacked partitions. Far worse was a total lack of bedding, which came about through an unfortunate mistranslation of the word *husbandry*. In English, the term applies strictly to agricultural implements, whereas the prospective settlers read in translation *Haushaltung*, implying that all manner of household items – everything from pots and pans to bedding – would be provided once they signed on. Consequently, prior to their voyage they sold all of their household goods. All passengers – men, women, and children alike – were buffeted about on bare boards throughout their laboured passage across the North Atlantic. This doubtless played a large part in the high death rate during the crossing.

Ann arrived in Halifax on Sunday, September 13, 1750, one year after the city's founding. After recovering from their epic voyage, the immigrants worked in the area to try to reduce the debt for their passage. The governor, Colonel Edward Cornwallis, impressed with the foreign Protestants, whom most English settlers mistook as Dutch, misinterpreting *Deutsch*, found work for many of them clearing land and constructing "musket-proof" log houses. Although not all of them were of peasant background, most were quite satisfied to find such rude employ. Others found work as craftsmen and soldiers in the King's forces.

At last, on May 28, 1753, over four hundred settlers embarked from Halifax for Merliguash, the future site of Lunenburg. They landed on June 8 at Rous's Brook, a convenient watering station for ships. Each received land allotments, generally thirty acres conveyed by warranty deed. In the lead-up to the Seven Years War in North America (1754-1763), the settlers then had no choice but to face up to the many challenges of their new life, among them echoes of unrest and civil strife which hounded them across the Atlantic.

Topping the list of terrors were the depredations by aboriginals of the (Catholic) Wabanaki Confederacy. Ardently allied with the French, they raided Lunenburg nine times during the first few years of its settlement, killing and scalping dozens of settlers. During the American Revolution, on July 1, 1782, six ships manned by American privateers sacked the town, having arrived in the night unseen by watchmen in charge of twelve-pounder alarm cannons mounted on various headlands outside of Lunenburg. Some of those cannon survived until recently on a hill in the woods north of Kingsburg Pond in Lower Kingsburg; two others from Five Houses lie to this day by the roadside in Lower LaHave.

Gudde Morje!
How is Vadder, how is Mudder,
how sin She, how sin Dechder?
Mer winsche eich en glicklich neies Yaahr,
Mer schdehe yetz uf eier Land
Mit unsre Flinde in der Hand.
Unsre Haahne sin geschbant.
Wann's eich dutt verdriesse,
Misst der's saage, eb mer schiesse.
Derweil mer heere ken Verdruss,
So sollt dir here unsern Schuss.

Greeting rendered in the Renish-Franconian dialect by Belsnickles on New Year's Eve in Lunenburg County. A rough English translation follows:

Good morning!
How is father, how is mother,
how are sons, how are daughters?
We wish you a Happy New Year,
We stand now on your land
With our rifles in the hand.
They are cocked and in tension.
If this does irritate you,
You must say it before we shoot.
If we hear of no irritation,
So you shall hear our shot.

"*Schiessen, oder nicht schiessen?* (Should we fire our guns or not?)" the *Belsnickles* likely sang out as Titus's mother Letitia laboured through the advent of the New Year, 1894. Similar to mummery, the old custom of *belsnickling* is derived from the term *Pelznickel* or *Belznickel*, which in Germany applied to a costumed figure carrying gifts for the Christ Child during Christmastime. Snowstorms, no matter how wild, never stopped *Belsnickles* from making their rounds – it was too much fun. But perhaps the reply that night was to please refrain from shooting due to the labour in progress.

Titus was born in the early hours of January 1, 1894, during a howling winter's gale. The New Year was ushered in amidst loud protests against the indignity of it all by the child delivered by mother Mary Ann Letitia (née Peeler).

Down on the shore, the spindrift-saturated wind roared off the rising tide with a vengeance. Driving ranks of unforgiving waves crashed upon the shore, carving a trademark steep winter beach profile. Spewing over that rocky barrier, the freezing mix sprayed the brackish waters of a broken line of bogs cringing in the lee not far from a line of higher ground inland. Rampaging in the blackness of night, the storm swept up and over a forest thick with stunted creaking spruce. A few miles to the west, the turbulent estuary of the LaHave River was frozen over almost up to Gaff Point. This winter was like a little Ice Age, though no one in Upper Kingsburg or anywhere else, for that matter, had ever heard of such a thing, much less named it so. Their winter ice road across the frozen river to markets in Bridgewater and LaHave patiently awaited trial by the weight of freight on local ox wagons.

The old homestead at the top of the hill shook as the wind wrestled everything within reach. Joining in nature's mad symphony, the storm windows played drummers, madly rattling and shaking in their fittings, their streaky bubble-laced glass masked by frost. From outside came the repeated, and curiously comforting, sweep of driven snow. Such was the setting for the opening act of our little protagonist's career on planet Earth.

"*Ein Junger!* (A boy!)" Grandma Peeler proudly pronounced. A well-respected midwife, she confidently grasped the child's legs and held him aloft for all to see. Moments later, the cord tied off, she slapped his bottom to get him started. Both she and Letitia's sister, Augusta, attended to the afterbirth and general cleaning up before Augusta rescued Papa Albert from the kitchen.

Letitia and Albert Mossman, Titus's parents, married in Lunenburg, June 1880.

This was Letitia's eighth delivery for the Mossman household. But there was no mistaking it – one would have thought that no one had ever had a child before, everyone was so pleased.

In so large a family it was not long before the child acquired a name. Papa Albert was quick to enter it in the huge leather-bound family Bible. "Titus Milton Mossman" it would be, although no precedent for this appears in the Mossman family tree. The tangle of names in that growth – more bush than tree – extended back already five generations in the New World.[1] Titus, like his six brothers and four sisters, was fated to take his place in a hardscrabble life that was the norm in large families of the time. To hear him tell it, Titus received no special treatment while growing up, except for regular brisk cuffs from his oldest bully brother Lemuel. He, first-born and fourteen years senior to Titus, was in line to inherit the homestead. Lemuel's siblings got used to taking orders.

Sundays were days of rest in Rose Bay and Kingsburg, particularly in this family, whose head was a lay preacher in the Presbyterian Church in Upper Rose Bay. Family diarists record that, to help pass Sunday afternoons during one winter, Titus and his young brothers Aubrey, Maurice, and Dennis played upstairs in the old house with their young cousin, Olive Louise. At the time Olive's mother (Flora Eldora) was away looking after Olive's father, who was ill with typhoid. Olive had a favourite rag doll as well as cut-out paper boats and paper dolls made for her by her father. She was also the proud owner of a doll's house. This was a large wooden box, in which the community mail order from Eaton's had arrived.

There was no telephone. Candles and kerosene lamps served as lights. Insulation was a combination of spruce boughs and seaweed. Plumbing consisted of a dug well and a two-seater outhouse beside the barn. Outdoor toilets were endured by many Maritime homeowners, including Titus and his

1 [1] David [2] Johannes [3] Abraham [4] Jacob [5] Albert and [6] Titus, counting twenty-five years for a generation.

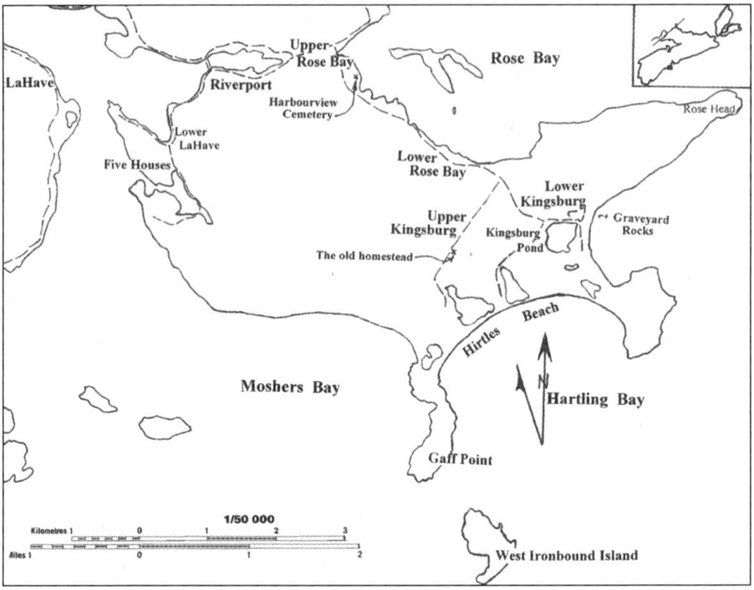

This map shows a portion of the South Shore, Lunenburg County, Nova Scotia, including Upper Kingsburg and "the old homestead" where Titus was born, West Ironbound Island, and other features and place names mentioned in the text.

wife, well into the 1940s. Titus's community was a conservative one of long standing, and neither he nor his wife was given to innovation when it came to living conditions. It was the early 1950s before they relented and installed a telephone.

Many communities in Nova Scotia existed in relative isolation in the late 1800s. Electronic gadgetry played no role. Tools and much equipment of the farming, fishing, and household trades were locally produced, as was – of course – nearly all of the food. Where doctors could be found, their relatively crude art provided the second-last word where human life hung in the balance. For numerous unfortunates, the scales tipped in favour of typhoid, polio, diphtheria, scarlet fever, or tuberculosis. Such was the lottery of endemic plagues lurking on the dark side of growing up pre-vaccines. Homes afflicted by tuberculosis were abandoned to decay, and shunned even by youngsters in search of adventure. They were warned against ever going into those old houses.

Times were hard, and life was accepted as such, none other being known to that generation. Their situation demanded resourcefulness and co-operation across the community. For adults, there was neither time nor the means to indulge at will in leisure activities.

Schooling for most children was a matter of family finances and luck, teachers being few and far between. Books and lessons appropriate to the ages of those assembled in the one-roomed schoolhouse at the foot of Vinegar Hill in Upper Kingsburg were largely acquired by chance. For fashioning the "three Rs" a piece of slate generally sufficed, there being no shortage of that commodity along the rocky South Shore of Nova Scotia. Depending upon farming and fishing duties, formal schooling for most children was brief. According to family legend, Titus graduated after three years, using some grade six books inherited along the way. In time, he proved himself surprisingly literate despite a hesitant scratchy script and poor reading ability.

Eleven mouths are a lot to feed. Like most young boys in early Nova Scotia coastal communities, Titus was encouraged to go to sea. However, at age thirteen, rather than stay at home shore fishing, he preferred to work as a flunkey on schooners shipping out of Lunenburg for the Grand Banks. On his first trips he went as either throater (cutting the throat and gutting the fish) or header (taking the heads off the fish). This was not a trivial assignment, especially in the days when an average cod forked on deck weighed twenty-five pounds and some twice that or more.

In brief, it was a school of hard knocks – and boys as young as ten years old worked beside him. Nor were those children given special consideration by older hands, for many of them were survivors of the same initiation. Some young fellows went over the side as full-fledged doryman at the age of thirteen, earning the princely sum of $1.50 per month. As recorded in my mother's sixteen-page pamphlet *Memories*, her brother Winfred Spindler was one such protégé. Titus may have done so as well. Children grew up fast in those days.

German (*Deutsch*) was once the dominant language in Lunenburg County. It may have helped that German-speaking Protestant ministers were among those appointed to various local circuits into the late 1800s. However, it was the primary language of only a very few households at the time of Titus's passing in 1974. In fact, the number of people claiming German descent in Nova Scotia decreased by about 30 percent after the Great War of 1914-1918, and yet again following the Second World War.

Titus, though rarely heard to speak German, retained a remarkable fluency in the language. According to my sister Carolyn, when she returned home with her husband in the early 1960s after several years of work and study in Switzerland, they were astonished to discover Titus had no difficulty conversing with them in German. More than likely he employed that talent to useful ends during his overseas deployment.

At home, however, any connection with Germany was conscientiously severed between the two world wars. One of our neighbours, a kindly elderly spinster (Nellie Colp), remarked to me when I was a child that in the early 1940s, while making her "trip of a lifetime" by train across Canada to see the Rocky Mountains, she and her cousin took great care not to be caught speaking German in public. Those same elders taught me simple rhymes and sayings in German which at the time I naively accepted as "Lunenburg Dutch."

By now all fluent native speakers of the German dialect spoken in Kingsburg and in Lunenburg County are extinct. That dialect is a variant form of Pennyslvania "Dutch" termed Renish-Franconian (*rheinfraenkisch*). The Pennsylvania dialect is still spoken and written in Lancaster County, Pennsylvania, and by Old Order Mennonites and Old Order Amish in the Waterloo region in Ontario. It is close to the dialect spoken around Mannheim and Worms on the Rhine.

However, only recordings remain of the songs and conversations once familiar to the people in Kingsburg, Lunenburg County. "*Grank, grank bin ich* (I am sick)" is one of the more popular old songs, portions of which were familiar to most locals in Titus's time. My sister Carolyn can still recite it by heart. It tells the story of a lovesick boy from Lunenburg County, rendered in a Nova Scotia version of the dialect by John Hirtle of Lower Kingsburg and recorded on tape by Manfred Richter about 1970. This and other old songs and sayings from Lunenburg County are archived at Deutsches Volksliedarchiv in Freiburg, Germany.

Grank, grank bin ich, vun Hazen iwwer nix,
Vun Hazen misseraawell, so grank bin ich.
Da kommet mei Vadder und besuchet mich,
Dann stell ich mich so hie
Und ich sag ihm meine Sinde.
Und du bist nich der letzte Bube
Grank's immer bin.

I am so sick at heart over nothing,
I'm miserable at heart, I'm so sick.
My father comes and visits me,
Then I stand up
And tell him about all my troubles.
(He tells me that) you're not the last young fellow
Who has ever been sick.

In Lower Kingsburg, John Hirtle, a direct descendent of Christian Hirtle (born 1774), loved singing that song. "Old" John Hirtle peeled many a ton of apples and homegrown potatoes for his daughter, Gladys. Her famous but humble – and now legendary – canteen perched precariously on the crest of Hirtle's Beach beside her home at the foot of the hill below Titus's birthplace. Gladee's Canteen opened for business in the mid-1950s. She was an outstandingly kind, proud, hard-working and hard-drinking proprietor. During the summer tourist seasons, interrupted from time to time by the devastation of hurricanes, Gladee's Canteen endured as a popular local landmark.

Gladys's sister Florence (Flossie), a compulsively compassionate woman, was also dedicated to hard work, as to family. As an excellent and prolifically productive cook, she helped run the canteen. A visiting tourist in 1972 estimated that Flossie's lifetime production of twelve-inch diameter pies baked during the canteen's summer seasons, laid side by side, would extend the twelve miles from Kingsburg Beach to the Lunenburg town hall. Incidentally, she was also able and willing to sing, with but little encouragement, many of the same songs that her father loved and remembered so well. Voted one of the ten best places to eat in Canada, the canteen closed for the last time in 1992. Flossie died in 1995 a full decade after Titus, and was the last of the generation who spoke the old dialect.

The early twentieth-century shore fishing in Lunenburg County, which Titus so assiduously avoided, was a labour of love for some, though it posed many risks. It was carried out in locally built wooden dories, seventeen to twenty-three feet long and powered by oar or sail. With luck, by catching an early morning offshore wind, the haul to the fishing grounds could be made entirely under sail. Ideally, the return trip would likewise harness onshore breezes generated around midday as cool air off the water rushes shoreward to replace warmer air rising off the land. More often than not, though, conditions were less than ideal. Failure of these winds left the hapless seaman no recourse but his oars. Upon regaining shore, however late in the day, the "make and mend" never let up.

Seasons for fishing were dictated by the fish, except in the dead of winter. Titus was familiar through short practice with the business because, along with small-scale farming, shore fishing was an integrated family affair. The annual laying in of a good supply of salted and properly flake-dried cod, along with the storage of root crops, the production of sauerkraut, and the cutting and storage of wood for fuel were markers of their way of life.

An account of the settlement in Lunenburg in 1761 reported that people were busily engaged in farming and showed little interest in fishing. This changed with the settlement of large numbers of sea-savvy New England Planters in 1760. Titus's ancestors began to respond to the call from the sea. Then, when British shipping policies were relaxed in the 1800s, colonials were allowed to build and crew their own ships. Given expanding markets, the merchant class sat up and took note. A shipbuilding boom commenced in the mid-1800s. Modelled on the work of Gloucestermen, the schooner was later perfected in that iconic Canadian ship the *Bluenose*, constructed in Smith and Rhuland's Lunenburg shipyard.

Competition was keen for a berth on a schooner, especially one skippered by a "high-liner" (successful) captain. Cooks were not hired on merit but rather by chance, and young Titus was simply told on one occasion by the hard-up captain that he would "have to be cook on this trip." There was no cooking school. He learned on the job. As matters turned out, Titus's main job in civilian life would be to serve as cook on various salt bankers. In this respect, his lack of education probably served to bond the man to the position, a situation which he eventually, if somewhat grudgingly, came to accept.

Hundreds of schooners were produced in Lunenburg shipyards. Wonderful sailing vessels on their own, they were incredibly stable in rough seas. However, the positive response to sail and helm was greatly reduced on return trips from the Grand Banks, with holds filled with "green" salted cod.

The long lists of names on the memorial plinths of polished gabbro on Lunenburg's waterfront are sober reminders of the price paid by many in the fishing indusry. The loss of a deckhand or two in the course of a trip, whether washed overboard or among the missing after a dory's failure to make it back to the ship after setting and/or hauling, was scarcely unusual. Nor were captains, whose word at sea was law, necessarily paragons of compassion and care. They were the ones who decided whether or not, and when, to launch the dories. Nor did a vessel aways return to port following the loss of a man. When it did, a flag was fixed "halfways to the cross," that is to say halfway down from the top of the mast to the crosstrees. Whereupon everyone on shore converged on the ship to find out what happened and who had been lost.

The posed postcard/photograph on page 31 of a teenaged Titus with a friend hints at shared good natures and a ready-for-anything attitude, as smiles fairly twitch for release beneath their forced attempt at seriousness. In real life, transformed from this parlour scene to experienced dorymen at work from a Grand Banks schooner, they were prepared to face the odds. Hard work, discipline, close calls, and calamities were the norm during the fishing season. All things considered, this was excellent basic training for Titus in view of his future status as a soldier.

This was a time well before the magic of radar, satellite-linked location devices, and fish-finding sonar. Hazards abounded. For example, Sable Island was a frequent source of grief to ships homeward bound under foggy conditions or driven off course during a hurricane. The island is a narrow sandbank about twenty-five miles long and up to a mile wide nestled loosely within a huge glacially scoured bedrock channel. Like a snake without a head, there is at each end a tail, which switches about from season to season according to the whim of winds and ocean currents. Uncertain of location, but hearing the roar of breakers to leeward, a captain might well pile on all sail in hopes of quickly getting past this

Fifteen-year-old Titus (seated) is flanked by a companion, identified as a fisherman with the surname of Greek from Blue Rocks.

"Graveyard of the Atlantic." The unlucky ones hit hard and the careers of crew and cargo alike were terminated.

Titus dodged this particular bullet on at least one occasion when his ship, striking twice, was bumped across the western tail of Sable during an August gale, starboard rail under, most hands gripped in fervent prayer onto stanchions or the nearest bit of rigging. A brief account of a similar event is given in Lunenburg's Fisheries Museum of the Atlantic, complete with a bottle of Sable's sand salvaged for posterity from shovelfuls cleared from a ship's deck.

By 1894 there already existed in the Mossman family memory numerous accounts of misadventure at sea. Israel Spindler recounts the wreck of the *Welcome* on August 29, 1883, as relayed by D. Luther Roth, pastor of Zion's Lutheran Church, Lunenburg, in the January 16, 1895, edition of the Lunenburg *Progress*:

I held on for 26 hours. How the night was spent, God only knows. Often I was asleep while clinging to the wreck. I was all over it, climbing around from place to place. I felt strong and vigorous, not at all tired, though often washed out at full length on the sea, holding with one hand while the muscles of my arm creaked with the strain. At last I was picked up by John Campbell and John MacAlee and then my strength was gone. I fell exhausted in the boat and have not yet recovered from the terrors of that dreadful scene.

Israel Spindler was the sole survivor. Israel's two sons, Alfred and Gabriel, and his brother William were among the ten fishermen lost during the wreck of the *Welcome*. All were local men. As a footnote to that episode, it is worth noting that Israel's family was the source of Titus's future wife Helen Viola Spindler. Life in those times was so precarious that one's ancestors were lucky to be born.

Titus and Helen Viola were married in September 1928. This milestone in their lives followed Titus's seven years schooling at sea and a decade after nearly four years of military service in the Canadian army, the last two of which saw him at the Front in France and Flanders.

2

Now We Wear the Feather

Now we wear the feather, the 85th feather,
We wear it with pride and joy,
That fake Advertiser, Old Billy the Kaiser,
Shall hear from each Bluenose boy.
Where trouble is brewing, our bit we'll be doing,
To hammer down Briton's foes,
With the bagpipes a-humming, the 85th's coming,
From the land where the maple leaf grows.

– *Songs of the 85th Overseas Battalion,*
Canadian Expeditionary Force (CEF)

Despite a century of hindsight there is no consensus on the root cause of the Great War. The trigger for the tragedy was predicted in 1888 by German statesman Otto von Bismarck, who remarked that "some damned foolish thing in the Balkans" would one day lead to a great European war. And so it was: on June 28, 1914, the heir to the Austro-Hungarian throne, Archduke Franz Ferdinand, and his wife Sophie, Duchess of Hohenberg, were shot by Gavrilo Princip, one of six Serb assassins. For years, the starting gun had been cocked and loaded with a complex mix of nationalism, territorial disputes, arms races, and a net of defensive alliances and rivalries for strength, prestige, and wealth among the Great Powers – the British Empire, the Austro-Hungarian Empire, Italy, France, Germany, and Russia.

The crisis reached full bloom in August 1914. History would be made very quickly, although in this instance, less easily explained. The world's record of wars and rumours of war highlights a wicked human predilection for conflict and battle. But this was a classic case of international brinkmanship which swiftly tipped out of the control of the instigators. As war got underway in 1914, the British Empire, France, and Russia (the so-called Triple Entente) found themselves confronting the Central Powers of Germany, Hungary and the Ottoman Empire.[1] The Western Front in France and Belgium, and the Eastern Front in Russia became the main theatres of the Great War.

A self-governing Dominion in the far-flung British Empire, Canada was automatically at war when Britain declared on August 13, 1914. At the time, Canada, with a population of less than eight million, had a professional permanent army of only about 3,000 full-time career soldiers. Canadians would remain British citizens until 1947, and this Canadian force thus fell under the command of the British Army.

The first wave of the British Expeditionary Force (BEF) made contact with their declared aggressor on August 22, 1914, at Mons, Belgium. It was the first battle of British troops on continental Europe since Waterloo, one century earlier. Two days later, with German forces about to overwhelm them, the British sounded a retreat. Already it was far too late for the politicians to even reconsider their decision to take up arms.

---

1 An *Entente Cordiale* between England and France and a separate "*entente*" between England and Russia were expressions of good will, friendly alliances rather than military alliances among these three Great Powers.

Meanwhile, and contrary to all expectations, the heavily outgunned and outnumbered Belgians, led by King Albert, were in the midst of a brilliant month-long opposition to the advancing German forces. By early October a million men were dead and the armies ground to a halt, confronting each other across a narrow No Man's Land between opposing trenches. Costs of future advances by either side were measured in thousands of dead, and, in some instances, tens of thousands per square mile.

The Great War was underway on the Western Front. Deservedly named for its unprecedented scale, in the words of Winston Churchill, "The Great War differed from all ancient wars in the immense power of the combatants and their fearful agencies of destruction, and from all modern wars in the utter ruthlessness with which it was fought. All the horrors of all the ages were brought together, and not only armies but whole populations were thrust into the midst of them."

In August 1914, while many sober folks regarded the prospect of war with pure horror, others – men and women alike – were wildly delighted. *In Sexual Life in the Great War*, Fischer and Dubois document in detail the extent of international fervour for war and the accompanying relaxation of moral restraints: "... the outbreak of war did not shock the conscience either of the men or of the women; more or less subconsciously, they welcomed it when it came. At last their primeval instincts were liberated from all the reserves and restraints of the past. War enthusiasm burst upon the world with sudden, overwhelming violence."

According to Pierre Berton in *Marching as to War*, thousands of celebrants in Canadian cities "marched through the streets singing and shouting exactly as they would during a spontaneous victory parade." The world, and particularly Europe, was in the midst of a profoundly unsettling transformation. The news of war triggered the expectation of a new age dawning, and led to a mix of passionate enthusiasm and suppressed anxiety, especially in young people. Germany was swept by euphoria as the troops marched off to war. In England, mathematician and philosopher Bertrand Russell was astonished to behold huge cheering crowds in Trafalgar Square. No one, anywhere, reckoned on the conflict lasting longer than three or four months at most.

Anticipating an early victory, the Germans stockpiled potassium nitrate (obtained from guano deposits in South America) adequate to meet their needs for manufacturing explosives for only six months. As matters turned out, they would need more, much more. Fortunately for them, by happy coincidence German chemist Fritz Haber discovered in 1909 how to fix nitrogen from the atmosphere in order to create ammonia, which is essential to the production of fertilizer and explosives. His tabletop demonstration was ramped up to industrial scale in 1913 by his colleague Carl Bosch at the Kaiser Wilhelm Institute of Chemistry in Berlin. Well positioned at the forefront of efforts to develop efficient delivery of explosives and chlorine gas to enemy trenches, Bosch pioneered high-pressure chemistry and founded a huge chemical company. Haber and Bosch won Nobel prizes in chemistry in 1918 and 1931 respectively.

The stakes were high for the nations involved, as were hopes for a short conflict. Britain wanted to preserve her Empire. The Germans would fight to establish dominance in Europe and to gain territory. It was to this end that the German General Staff drafted the Schlieffen Plan in 1899. This plan violated Belgian sovereignty to quickly access France and was in clear contravention of the 1839 international treaty recognizing Belgian neutrality by France, England, Russia, Prussia, and Austria. Meanwhile, the French were building up a huge army in hopes of regaining Alsace-Lorraine, which they had lost to Germany in the Franco-Prussian War of 1870-1871. Myriad thick fogs of war were quickly developing along diverse fronts: Western, Eastern,

Gallipoli, Italian, Palestine, Mesopotamian, African, and the Far East – not to mention the conflict at sea.

It is in this context that Titus, like several other young men in his community, enlisted in Lunenburg on October 7, 1915. This date is recorded in his Regimental Pay Book as his "Attestation Date." In England, any healthy young men out of uniform were publicly embarrassed by white feathers given to them by young women. At that time and in that place, there was no mistaking the symbol. It was a sign that the recipient was considered a coward. But Titus was in no way under pressure to join up. Conscription was over a year and a half in the future.

The 85th Canadian Infantry Battalion, one of many units in the Canadian Expeditionary Force (CEF), was already three weeks old, having been authorized on September 14, 1915, upon appointment of its Commanding Officer Lt. Col. Allison H. Borden, brother of the Prime Minister of Canada, Sir Robert Laird Borden. Robert Borden (1854-1937) was born in Grand Pré, Kings County, Nova Scotia, and was prime minister from 1911 to 1920. As the Great War progressed he would increasingly insist that Canada become an autonomous nation in the field of international diplomacy.

Three weeks later the battalion relocated to the Halifax Armouries for mobilization in the midst of a vigorous recruitment program. As part of this program, on February 14, 1916, Lt. Col. Borden would send a letter to "the boys and girls of Nova Scotia schools" asking them "to carry this letter home and show it to your father and big brothers, and you can ask them to come with me and other grown up Nova Scotia school boys in the defense of Nova Scotia, Canada, and the Empire."

On October 14, 1915, mobilization officially took place at the Halifax Armouries. The die was cast. 222568 Rifleman Mossman was destined to serve overseas in the 85th Canadian Infantry Battalion, Nova Scotia Highlanders. The photo on page 39 shows Titus rigged out in his fancy new uniform,

Titus, relaxed and rigged out in his army uniform in October 1915, shortly after joining up, poses with his brother Josiah Irvin, and (standing) William (Willy) Lohnes, a neighbour.

posed with sober-faced brother Josiah and friend Willy Lohnes in a Lunenburg studio. A faint smile plays on Titus's face, almost as if he can't quite believe the commitment he's made. He is a healthy, sturdily built lad of twenty-one. Of his six brothers, only Dennis, the second youngest child in the family, joined up, and that in the navy.

Province-wide, 25,118 men were accepted for duty overseas. Drawn from various parts of Nova Scotia, the four companies of the 85th Canadian Infantry Battalion and their complement of over 1,000 men were A (Pictou, Cumberland, and Colchester counties), B (Lunenburg, Queens, Shelburne, Yarmouth, Digby, Annapolis, Antigonish, and Guysborough counties), C (Halifax, Hants, and Kings counties), and D (Cape Breton Island).

Upon mobilization on October 14, 1915, the assembled raw recruits, a motley-clad mass of civilians from all walks of life, were viewed by army staff on Day One with thinly disguised distaste. A high percentage of these volunteers could neither read nor write. In very short order they found themselves quartered in either the Armouries (A Company) or in tents on the Halifax Commons. Equipment was issued, and basic training began.

This instruction, in close to classic British military style, was as exacting in discipline when it came to dress as it was to the finer points of hand-to-hand conflict. Its lightest aspects are found in the routine requirements that buttons and boots must be properly polished. In the trenches during the Great War too, a filthy button or failure to salute properly could merit punishment. The practice carried over from the eighteenth century when it was considered by the governing class that a man could be completely molded by insistent repetitious indoctrination. Deeply rooted in the English caste system, its worst expression is aptly described as sado-masochistic. A champion of this art, General Douglas Haig ascended to Commander-in-Chief of the BEF in December 1915.

Part of a large panoramic photograph of the 85th Battalion cropped to feature B Company on the Halifax Commons in November 1915. The Armouries is in the background on the left. On the left a portion of A Company borders B Company and on the right is a small part of C Company. D Company is out of view at the far right.

Leisure time at this early stage of basic training was limited to church parade. Titus may well have considered it leisure time, but I can attest that, postwar, it was never his first choice. In his civilian life, his preference on Sundays was always to remain at home and stand watch as dinner cooked, while the rest of the family went to Sunday school and church. The latter function was usually a double header, with morning and evening service.

An approximate head count from an official wide-angle photograph in Titus's archives shows 829 men (several men are hidden behind horses) of the four companies of the 85th Battalion lined up at attention in their heavy khaki greatcoats on the Halifax Common (generally referred to as "the Commons") in late November 1915. Horse-mounted officers are stationed front and centre, and to either side (only B Company is shown here). Everyone is wearing gloves.

Long shadows show that it is late afternoon. The trees are leafless. An aura of accomplishment within the ranks is almost palpable. After all, the portrait captures a sort of graduation ceremony. There is a lot going on here.

Facing west, the soldiers' rifle butts are placed exactly on a white-chalked line drawn along the ground for this purpose. This is, after all, one of many early lessons on the importance of lines (and discipline) for soldiers. Magnification of the original photograph reveals a few smiles, but most recruits already realize that smiling while on parade is not an army tradition. Above many upper lips, thin, trim "toothbrush" moustaches (as recommended by the army) have already appeared.

The 85th Battalion was unusually fortunate in having a fine marching and symphonic brass and reed band. Its forerunner was the old Albion Mines Band, which was established in Stellarton during the 1840s. Although military bands were considered good for morale in camp during rest and while training, it was not usual for them to accompany an active fighting unit to the Front. However, when the time came to cross to France, the Commanding Officer of the 85th Battalion solved the problem by blending the bandsmen in with the "fighting men" and by safely packing away all musical instruments within the Quartermaster's stores.

In the photograph showing B Company, the protruding tubas, trombones, big brass drums, and the white-tipped pipes (drones) of bagpipes betray the presence of musicians within the ranks. And near the back row, a yard or so to the right, a well-trained short-eared white terrier (the battalion mascot perhaps?) sits patiently, at attention.

Behind the serried ranks, a scattering of onlookers, mostly male, includes some young boys hoping no doubt to see some action. Distanced behind the battalion, and enclosed behind a wire fence to the northeast, are several long huts, which would be home to the troops for the next six months. Between the battalion and the fenced-off housing compound, several small groups of citizens are going about their business. Well acquainted with the comings and goings of soldiers, they make their way obliquely across the Commons along one of several well-established footpaths.

In that sea of mostly sober faces, family members argue that Titus stands eighth in from the left (as the photo is viewed) in the fourth row in B Company. Close to anonymity and safe in this setting from unequivocal identification, this former seaman was now a number. He answered to "222568 Rifleman Mossman, Sir!" of the 85th Overseas Battalion, Canadian Expeditionary Forces (CEF). Chosen on the advice of a Gaelic scholar in Antigonish, the motto of the battalion was *Siol Na Fear Fearail* (The Breed of Manly Men). Of the four companies only D Company consisted of troops from Cape Breton Island. Some of the men in B Company had, at best, exceedingly thin Highland blood.

No matter their background, all troops in the 85th were encouraged to learn particular songs (including some in Gaelic) from a small booklet especially prepared for use by the Nova Scotia Highlanders. "The 85th Feather" may have fit the very early days of routine army propaganda and repetitious instruction, but I have never heard it sung. Although scarcely as memorable as the equally anonymous "Farewell to Nova Scotia" (one of many treasured Nova Scotia songs collected by folklorist Helen Creighton), some critics may see a touch of irony in King George V's calling to arms and in the same breath taking swipes at his cousin "Old Billy," the Kaiser.

I used to walk the sidewalk in a Nova Scotia town,
There was a man came down, his face was bronzed and brown,
He told us how King George was calling each to do his share,
He offered us a khaki coat to wear.
He told us how the call had gone far over land and sea,
And when I heard that speaker's word,
I said, "Why that means me."

(Chorus)
Now we wear the feather, the 85th feather,
We wear it with pride and joy,
That fake Advertiser, Old Billy the Kaiser,
Shall hear from each Bluenose boy.

Where trouble is brewing, our bit we'll be doing,
To hammer down Briton's foes,
With the bagpipes a-humming, the 85th's coming,
From the land where the maple leaf grows.

And when we've put the Kaiser where he cannot ride or roam,
We'll beat it straight for home, across the raging foam;
Where every pretty girl we meet will greet us with a smile,
They'll not forget, but wait for us a while;
And never were such lassies, so sweet, so fair, so true,
A welcome warm as sunshine waits our boys when they get through.

And when for King and Country we shall all have done our bit,
And safe at home we sit, when Kaiser Bill has quit,
We'll tell how sons of Canada for country did and dared,
The glory Borden's fighting Gamecocks shared.
And though the years may find our boys in far and distant lands,
In memory how often we shall clasp our comrades' hands.

The reference to "Borden's fighting Gamecocks" in "The 85th Feather" alludes to the Highlanders' khaki woolen Balmoral cap bearing two small red feathers in front of three larger cock feathers, all held in place by the cap badge. The choice of gamecocks to characterize soldiers in the 85th Battalion has a great deal to recommend it. The spirit of those birds very closely describes that of brave men putting their lives at risk when thrown into the pit of combat.

Training continued throughout the fall and winter of 1915-1916 in Halifax. Then, in May 1916, the entire 4th Brigade (close on 7,000 soldiers) moved from the Halifax Commons to Camp Aldershot in the beautiful Annapolis Valley, Nova Scotia. Named after the British Army training facility in Aldershot, Hampshire, England, this 2,810-acre military camp is well suited for military training, being situated in a pine forest interspersed with sand dunes and clumps of juniper.

Camp Aldershot, Annapolis Valley, summer 1916 – courtesy of Bruce MacDonald's blog World War I Veterans of Guysborough County.

Abutting a railway to Halifax, it was convenient, too, for transporting troops and supplies.

That summer of 1916, through to the fall, the troops were housed in canvas tents, with temporary buildings serving as hospital, cookhouses, and messes. Their training went on relentlessly. By early fall, each of the approximately 5,000 men in the Nova Scotia Highland Brigade had been marched to especially erected studios to have their official photograph recorded. But, without doubt, the highlight of their stay at Camp Aldershot occurred on September 26, 1916, when, as the brigade's senior unit, the 85th Battalion received their Colours from Lady Borden, wife of the Prime Minister of Canada. Finally, more than a year after the battalion's creation, the troops took a train to Halifax in October 1916 to board a ship for the transatlantic crossing. Titus was promoted while at Aldershot and now answered as "222568 Lance Corporal Mossman" when collecting his pay as rifleman in the 85th Battalion.

Troops crowd the decks as the *Olympic* approaches England. The view from a seaplane shows two stern chasers (guns) and dazzle camouflage colours used to confuse the enemy as to her speed and heading. Image by W.E. Axten, Publisher, Southampton. Courtesy Nova Scotia Highlanders Regimental Museum, Amherst, Nova Scotia.

3

One of Three Sisters

... her cargo remained the same on every voyage since the beginning of the war: three bars of khaki lining the rails, five thousand Canadians travelling in bond, going to Europe with nothing to declare.

– RMS Olympic's departure for England December 6, 1917 in Barometer Rising by Hugh MacLennan

On arrival in Halifax on Wednesday, October 11, 1916, Titus and his comrades in arms, in total 34 officers and 1,015 "other ranks," were greeted by the sight of the gigantic White Star Royal Mail Steamer *Olympic*. A four-stacker, it had arrived on October 8 and stood by, awaiting boarding by several battalions, including the 85th. This huge, relatively new ship of His Majesty's Transport was destined to survive the war, retiring in 1935, and to thoroughly earn its nickname, "Old Reliable."

Measuring 882 feet 6 inches in length, *Olympic* was identical to RMS *Titanic*; both were built side by side in Belfast, Ireland, in Harland and Wolff's shipyards. *Olympic* was launched on October 20, 1910, before *Titanic*, and her maiden voyage from Liverpool to New York began on June 14, 1911. A third and slightly larger sister ship, *Britannic*, was planned at her launching in 1914 to be the world's finest passenger liner.

Britannic did not realize her potential as a passenger liner. She was swiftly requisitioned by the government early in the war to serve as His Majesty's Hospital Ship. Her fatal sixth and final voyage was to Moúdros, on the Greek island of Lemnos, to collect casualties from the calamitous conflict raging in the Dardanelles. Mercifully, most of her 3,300 hospital beds were unoccupied. *Britannic* is believed to have struck a mine off the island of Kea in the Aegean Sea, and sank in fifty-five minutes at about 9:00 a.m. on November 21, 1916. Aboard was Violet Jessop, an English nurse who survived a 1911 collision of *Olympic* with a British warship, the sinking of the *Titanic* in 1912, and the 1916 plunge of the *Britannic* to the bottom of the sea.

With sixty-one-year-old Captain E.J. Smith at the helm, *Olympic*'s maiden voyage was relatively uneventful except for a single incident. While docking in New York on June 21, 1911, the powerful thrust of one of her outboard wing propellers damaged and nearly sank one of the tugboats. Three months later a more serious incident occurred off the Isle of Wight, when the ship collided with the British warship HMS *Hawke*, thoroughly bashing in the prow of the cruiser. Although one of her propeller shafts was twisted and two of her waterproof compartments destroyed, *Olympic* managed to limp back to Southampton. The Royal Navy blamed *Olympic* for the accident, but Captain Smith retained ascendant status in the White Star Line. Others in the sailing business were not as charitable, viewing these accidents as bad omens for the forthcoming maiden voyage of the *Titanic* which, despite his now somewhat tarnished record, would be captained by Smith.

As matters turned out, repairs to *Olympic* required some cannibalizing of *Titanic*'s body parts (for example, one drive shaft) in order to keep *Olympic* up and running. Consequently, *Titanic*'s sailing date was postponed from March 20 to April 10, 1912. Her fate lay in ambush among the prowling iceberg packs off Newfoundland's continental shelf.

Following the April 15, 1912, sinking of the *Titanic*, the *Olympic* underwent an extensive refit. Equipped with two 15,000 b.h.p. (brake horse power) reciprocating engines driving outboard wing propellers, and one 16,000 b.h.p. low-pressure turbine driving one propeller amidships, *Olympic* was capable of hours-long sustained speed of 23 knots; her record speed of 27.81 knots stood for many years.

Certainly speed helped her evade the far slower U-boats of the day, which could attain a maximum speed of eight knots under water and which, by mid-1915, had begun to take a serious toll on Allied shipping. *Olympic* was also outfitted with two 4.7-inch guns at the bow and two stern chasers. Apart from reliability, by the end of the war she gained the added distinction of being the only merchant ship to destroy a U-boat – U-103 – and that by ramming, on the morning of May 12, 1918, while en route to France with a complement of American soldiers.

Starting in mid-September 1915, *Olympic* made twelve trips eastward across the Atlantic in her role as a Canadian troopship. Among her other trips were eight carrying American troops and two carrying members of the Chinese Labour Battalion. On return trips to Halifax, she conveyed convalescent casualties. Her captain throughout the war, Bertram (Bertie) Fox Hayes, argued successfully to have *Olympic* sail alone at her regular cruising speed of 22 knots, rather than in convoy at a leisurely 12 knots.

Olympic's eighth arrival in Halifax on October 1, 1916, was characteristically a very difficult one for returning wounded Canadians. This was because of the callous practice, regardless of weather, of disembarking the critically wounded so-called "cot cases" onto "lighters," or small boats, before the ship docked at Pier 2. Following the practice of ambulance trains being unloaded in London at night, the idea may have been to divert the public's attention from the number of seriously injured. Fortunately, a specific complaint registered by a local official, to the effect that even a sick cat shouldn't be treated like that, led to all future landings of wounded men being made after the ship docked.

On this, her eighth sailing to England, *Olympic* would carry an official complement of about 6,014 troops. Unfortunately, due to a major miscommunication on October 11, the 85th Battalion missed an opportunity to say godbye to friends and relatives assembled on the Halifax Commons. Unaware of that arrangement, the men marched directly to Pier 2 and boarded the ship. To their considerable rage, and that of many folks on shore, they were not allowed off again. Few men got another chance before sailing to see their loved ones.

On the way up the gangplank each soldier was given a card explaining exactly where his bed was located and the seating arrangement for meals. Like his comrades, Titus was impressed at the tremendous size of Old Reliable. He did allow, however, that "below decks we was squeezed together pretty tight, all in rope hammocks. Must o' been a t'ousand or more of us, packed together like sardines in a tin, hardly room to put anyt'ing. A man had way more room in a schooner."

Reports about *Olympic* at this particular time confirm this brief observation that accommodation for soldiers below decks was rather less than third class. Altogether cramped and claustrophobic, their hammocks were close-packed to the roof with next to no space left for kit. According to David Gray[1], meals were of good quality, although eating quarters were rough.

---

1 David Gray, "Carrying Canadian Troops: The Story of RMS Olympic as a First War World Troopship," in *Canadian Military History* vol. 11, #1, 2002.

U-boat *Deutschland*, the first submarine to cross the Atlantic Ocean, shown arriving in Baltimore, Maryland, on July 10, 1916. Built at Bremen as a merchant craft, it was 315 feet long and carried a crew of 29 and 750 tons of cargo at a maximum speed of 8 knots underwater or 18 knots on the surface.

These were exciting times, no doubt about it. However, word was now received that departure would be delayed for two days. "Hurry up and wait" was by now a byword in the ranks. There were reports of a U-boat in the area. To an enemy submarine, any ship the size and importance of *Olympic* was a prime target. Only three months earlier in July 1916, the unarmed merchant submarine *Deutschland* arrived in the neutral USA to the whistles and toots of steamers as they passed on Chesapeake Bay. (The United States did not enter the war until April 1917.) On shore, the Americans treated the genial Captain Koenig and his crew with the utmost hospitality. On this visit, his ship filled her holds with 402 tons of crude rubber and 95 tons of tin. One of seven such ships designed initially to carry cargo between the United States and Germany, Captain Koenig's *Deutschland* would soon

The *Olympic* preparing to leave Pier 2, Halifax, on October 13, 1916, with more than 5,000 men, including Titus Mossman and the 85th Battalion, on board. (Photograph by Cyril Ratchford of Amherst, Nova Scotia, who joined the 85th on November 6, 1917.)

be converted into a long-range cruiser – a predator fitted with very big teeth – in the so-called U-Kreuzer Flotilla.

Early Friday morning, October 13, 1916, *Olympic* cast off from her berth to lie at anchor in Bedford Basin all day long. Watching and being watched around the shore were crowds of people, among whom were several young ladies who could "wig wag" quite well, according to one young signaller on board. In the outer harbour, two armed merchant cruisers, the *Calgarian* and *Drake*, waited to escort the *Olympic* for the first couple of hundred miles.

4

Witley Camp

Canadian soldiers have subscribed £77 as a gift to the Church. It will be spent on oak paneling round the south side of the nave, which will bear a brass plate with the words: To the glory of God this oak paneling was placed in this ancient Church of the Motherland by Canadians in Witley Camp, 1918.

– The Church of All Saints pamphlet
E.J. Newell

With little fanfare *Olympic* weighed anchor at dusk on October 13, 1916, and was soon at sea, lights out. As weather permitted, various fatigue parties to swab decks and stairs were organized for those soldiers with sea legs. Likewise, each day there was some physical drill. Titus had little trouble with this routine.

Escorting destroyers met *Olympic* just over six days later, on her approach to the British Isles. Arriving early in Liverpool on October 19, 1916, the brigade got underway immediately to Witley Camp, arriving there in the evening. One of four Canadian camps located near Guildford[1], close to the Great Imperial Training Centre of Aldershot in South Surrey, Witley was mainly an infantry camp, though it also hosted the Reserve Artillery, the instruction for which was provided by the Canadian School of Gunnery.

To no one's surprise, army routine was promptly reestablished amidst high expectations of soon seeing action. After all, it is this latter prospect that most soldiers live in hopes of realizing, however much their loved ones may fail to understand. To the despair of these Canadian soldiers, though, it would be another four months of ceaseless drill before they would set foot in France. For army administrators, the problem of logistics and transport was as real here in England as it had been back in Canada.

At this point the 85th Battalion had been in basic training for over sixteen months since mobilization. That is an incredible length of time, considering that the process of basic training in most armies seldom lasts longer than six months. By this time the men were saturated with morale and spoiling for a fight. They had thoroughly morphed from down-home folks into men with a will to kill if they had to, for whatever cause perceived to be their mandate.

During those four long months at Witley, compulsory attendance at the nearby ancient Church of All Saints provided a bit of distraction from time to time for the soldiers. For example, they learned that the first account of Witley Church appears in the Domesday Book (1081 AD), which told William the Conqueror who owed him exactly what in taxes. The church, they were told, although structurally modified, is the same one that was there before the Norman Conquest in 1066. But divine services at Witley in early 1917 did little to ease the men's anxiety. To many, it seemed the war would be over and done with before they could take part.

---

1 The other three camps were Bramshott, Borden, and Seaford.

On Sunday, February 4, 1917, the battalion fell in at 1:00 p.m. and marched to the church, B Company having the honour of escorting the Colours. The 85th was shipping out! Their Colours would hang in the nave on the south side of the church until they returned to claim them at war's end.

As matters turned out, the 85th Canadian Infantry Battalion (Nova Scotia Highlanders) was the only one of the four battalions in the 12th Brigade permitted by higher British command to enter the war as a coherent unit. The other three battalions – the 185th, the 193rd and the 219th, to the intense dismay of those troops – were scheduled due to "military exigencies" to be assigned to supplying reinforcements for British units already at the front. This was disheartening news, especially delivered so close to dispatch time to the battlefields of France and Flanders.

While immersed in army drills at Witley, Titus learned that on January 3, 1917, his father had fallen dead in the snow four thousand miles away in a Nova Scotia forest. Papa Albert was on his way to lead the regular Wednesday prayer meeting in the Presbyterian Church in Upper Rose Bay. Being winter, the meeting was probably held in the morning. His favourite route to church from his home in Upper Kingsburg was a four-mile shortcut through the spruce woods.

Family diarists record that when Papa Albert failed to show up at church on January 3, the prayer meeting was cancelled and everyone turned out for the search. Tracked down by tell-tale signs in the snow, his crumpled body was located along the trail which passed close beside the home of his second son, Norman Albert Matthias. Exact cause of his death is not known. One of four boys in a family of eleven children, Albert was seventy years old. Diarists mention that he had been extremely upset when Titus joined the army and went off to war. Albert's concern was well founded because disturbing stories about the tragedy on the Somme were filtering through to the home front.

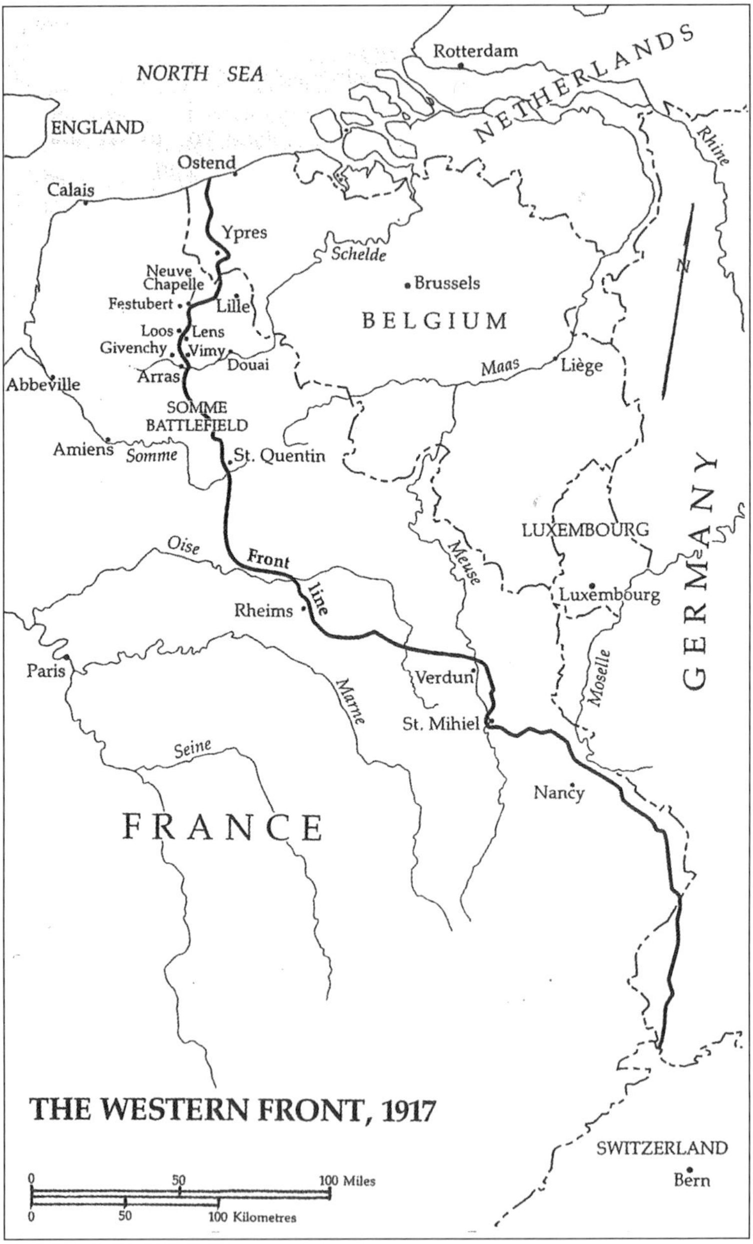

The Western Front, 1917; modified after Berton (1986:46).

PART II

IN THE LINE

5

Trench Warfare

'Good-morning; good-morning!' the General said
when we met him last week on our way to the line.
Now the soldiers he smiled at are most of 'em dead,
and we're cursing his staff for incompetent swine.
'He's a cheery old card,' grunted Harry to Jack
as they slogged up to Arras with rifle and pack.
But he did for them both by his plan of attack.

– "The General,"
Collected Poems 1908-1956
Siegfried Sassoon

I*m Westen Nichts Neues* (*All Quiet on the Western Front*) might well have served as the official German war news bulletin describing conditions at the outset of 1917. There had been no major battle on the Western Front for almost three months. The initial year-long German siege of Verdun and its ring of ancient forts, the longest battle (February 1914 to December 1915) of the war, ended in stalemate. This seemed to set the pattern for mutual destruction of opposing armies; at Verdun, there were half a million casualties on each side, French and German. Six months later, a mere ten miles to the west, the Battle of the Somme (July 1 to November 18, 1916) duplicated the butcher's bill.

General Sir Douglas Haig, appointed by Prime Minister Henry Asquith as the supreme Commander-in-Chief of the British Expeditionary Force (BEF), was duly authorized by fellow warlords to mount an offensive for a military breakthrough. In this role he made no secret of the fact that he was aided by "the Divine." Unfortunately for the Allies, at this point in the war the Germans held all the high ground, and a critical advantage in terms of weaponry. The armament imbalance came about, and persisted for years, primarily because of Haig's underestimation of the offensive powers of the machine gun. He considered it an overrated weapon.

On faith that infantrymen could defeat machine guns, Haig condemned the Allied forces under his command to repeat the same fatal mistakes over and over again. Berton notes that Haig is on record stating his belief that bullets had "little stopping power against the horse." As an old cavalryman, experience ought to have taught Haig otherwise.

Machine guns of various types were used to good effect by both sides during the Second Boer War (1899-1902), in which Haig served with such distinction that he was promoted to the War Office. He was also a staff officer at Omdurman in the Sudan in 1898 when the British, at a cost of forty-eight dead, destroyed with Maxim guns over 10,000 Sudanese. The wisdom of Hilaire Beloc's rhyme "Whatever happens, we have got the Maxim gun and they have not" seems to have been utterly lost on Haig. It is difficult, but nonetheless important, to try to comprehend the nature and scale of disconnects in Haig's thinking and his resultant criminal decisions which the BEF was forced to endure.

By the close of 1915, the British still had only two machine guns for each 12,000-man division compared to the Germans' fifty for 10,000 men. This simple discrepancy accounts for hundreds of thousands of BEF casualties. In early 1916, after almost two years of fighting, Haig continued his efforts to limit the number of machine guns given to battalions in the belief this would help maintain men's offensive grit. Fortunately, David Lloyd George, minister of munitions at the outbreak of war, became prime minister in December 1916, and insisted on increasing the number of machine guns.

Haig also argued against the use of steel helmets. Difficult as it is to believe, soldiers on both sides during the first year or so of the Great War wore caps made of either cloth (generally wool) or leather. A fancy spike-topped leather model (*Pickelhaube*) was standard equipment for German troops early in the war. Such was the influence of Germany's military that several countries, including the United States (1872) and England (1878), adopted something similar. That was before trench warfare became the fashion.

The Germans soon discovered the spike conferred no advantage whatsoever to a soldier making his way up the line through a trench system; on the contrary, the garnish atop the *Pickelhaube* directed the fickle finger of every potential sniper on the lookout for the enemy. Fresh German troops wearing new steel helmets and arriving at the Front in October 1916 guarded their new helmets very carefully lest they be exchanged for the older models.

The *Pickelhaube* might have earned the Germans their nickname of Huns as a spiked hat was also worn by Attila and his Huns. Moreover, Kaiser Wilhelm II – "Old Billy" – reportedly urged his soldiers to "fight like Huns!" when he sent them as part of the eight-nation alliance to help relieve the western embassies in Peking during the Boxer Rebellion (1898-1901). Billy and George were on far friendlier terms in those days. A third possible explanation of the term is the motto *Gott mit uns* inscribed on German belt buckles.

Spikey helmet or not, over the top they went, into No Man's Land. Allied troops advanced at a walking pace, in waves usually less than three hundred feet apart, the men in each wave spaced about six feet from each other. Their caps of course provided no protection from shrapnel shells exploding overhead; steel helmets were issued to the BEF in early 1916. Nevertheless, the practice of shearing soldiers' hair short in order to better treat head wounds has endured.

That British-led offensive on the Somme was, by any measure, an appalling disaster. And it was recognized as such by Allied soldiers, although they were absolutely powerless to do much about it. Their souls, along with civil rights and freedom, were surrendered when they signed up. The military demands blind obedience, and takes virtually total control over the lives of soldiers.

The 1916 Battle of the Somme, which involved twelve separate major actions between July 1 and November 18, holds the record for the largest number of battlefield casualties in a single day's action during the Great War – 58,000: one-third of them fatalities, and all for little if any gain. Morality aside, had the artillery been more effective, and if German barbed wire not been so thick and strong as to defy the best efforts of British wire cutters, opening day might have been a bit different. But it's doubtful. Even tanks, a "male" version (bearing two cannon) and a "female" version (bearing four machine guns), developed in great secrecy and introduced by the British on the Somme, made little difference following an initial scare for the Germans.

Opening day proved tragic indeed. On July 1, 1916, the 1st Newfoundland Regiment, a battalion in the British 29th Division, 88th Brigade, was but one of many groups of men ordered to advance, without artillery support, across No Man's Land at a walking pace, in slow-moving waves sixty to three hundred feet distant from each other, only to be mowed down in senseless slaughter. As Kevin Major makes clear in *No Man's Land*, the Newfoundlanders were granted no opportunity to acclimatize.

After a long march, they arrived at their assigned sector in the front line trenches at Beaumont Hamel about 2:30 a.m. before going over to meet their death later that same morning. There was no supporting artillery bombardment. Having received little, if any, briefing they were further handicapped by carrying, all uphill, over sixty-six pounds of marching kit including ammunition, flares, rations, trenching shovel, gas mask, empty sandbags, and barbed wire cutters that couldn't cut the German wire. They faced an impossible tactical situation in which German machine guns were permanently trained on the few gaps that existed in the wire. It was all over in thirty minutes. Of 801 men of the regiment, 733 were killed or severely wounded. Huge fan-shaped pileups of dead and wounded in front of the gaps told the sad story. The sounds and sights of those fields of carnage defy description.

Evidently General Haig preferred working at a distance and is said to have never been to the front line, or in a trench. According to Wade Davis in *Into the Silence*, "In four years, at the head of the largest army the British Empire had ever placed in the field, a force that would suffer 2,568,834 casualties in France and Belgium alone, Haig never once saw the front; nor did he visit the wounded."

In what amounted to a case of serial mass murder, Haig insisted on extending the ghastly initial push for ten successive days. Well over three weeks later the carnival of death on the Somme continued. The blood-letting persisted nearly five months. Unlike some of the wars currently underway, correspondents were barred from the Front during the Great War. Even so, stunning casualty lists appeared in the London *Times* and the *Toronto Star* each day. For example, the July 24, 1917, London *Times* listed 608 British officers as casualties with 156 dead, and 5,500 casualties of other ranks.

Davis comments, "Haig could not call off the Somme attack without admitting failure on a murderous scale. Therefore, he redefined the goals of the campaign and declared that attrition rather than military breakthrough had always been his intent." Throughout the campaign he played down the losses, saying "there was reason to believe" Allied casualties were less than those of the Germans.

Long before he assumed the reins of power following Asquith's resignation as prime minister on December 5, 1916, Lloyd George had been deeply distrustful of Haig's judgment. The politician's critical mind and receptiveness to fresh ideas resulted in well-documented instances of friction with Haig's rigidness and stubborn nature. Many of these occasions are matters of historical record. Examples of Lloyd George's "oft-quoted remarks" supplied by Pierre Berton are typical of the Prime Minister's contempt: "Haig does not care how many men he loses." And, "We could certainly beat the Germans if only we could get Haig to join them."

Nearly a decade later, Field Marshall Sir Douglas Haig, the "Great Man," stood on Duckworth Street in St. John's on July 1, 1924, to unveil the Newfoundland National War Memorial. King George V had promoted him to Field Marshall in January 1917 "as a New Year's gift from myself and the country." One must applaud the profoundly forgiving spirit of Newfoundlanders and their loyalty to the Motherland. Since Newfoundland did not join Confederation until 1949, "Canadians" did not officially take part in that infamous initial Allied offensive; only later did they participate in Haig's "Big Push" on the Somme.

As for the role of a divinity in the works, evidence of that belief abounds on both sides, from the top rung of authority to the bottom. General Haig considered himself God's servant and urged that clergymen be sent to the Front to remind men the war dead were martyrs for a grand cause. And so it continued, down into the lowermost chaplain ranks. Bishops and evangelists alike viewed the Germans as enemies of God. The German attitude, of course, was a mirror image of the Allies. Protestants, Roman Catholics, and Jews, in the ranks on both sides, were instructed to believe God was on their side in the battle.

It has been argued that war on the Western Front was a kind of religious thing, a holy war really, a crusade but without infidels and with few holds barred. The comment of my

Belgian friend Piet de Roose is likely closer to the truth: "It was madness." And here's the thing: how can anyone place their faith in any religion which insists in the name of peace, or worse, some deity, that they must attack and kill other people?

As background to Titus's story, one must realize that life in the trenches was one of unmitigated squalor. Legions of innocent, enthusiastic young men who joined the army to see the world expected to play a part in the heroics of war in a distant land. Instead, while awaiting death themselves, they saw comrades receive horrific wounds or torn apart during bombardments while crouching terrified and absolutely helpless in unspeakably filthy trenches. An even greater terror than sheltering in the trenches was the moment they would be ordered out and over the top. Framing their probable fate in either event was the smell of death and of fear – an overall stench of sweat, vomit, blood, and putrefying carcasses in their thousands, gangrene, and the mess of overflowing latrines. In warm weather, bluebottle flies buzzed about everywhere in swarms. Existing for days or weeks at a time half underground in these conditions, men were easy targets for the spread of disease.

Sharing the trenches with the men were millions of black and brown rats, allowing little rest at night and eating anything they could find, including wounded soldiers lying helpless and inaccessible out in No Man's Land. Especially feared and loathed were so-called brown "corpse rats," which gorged on protein-rich portions of human remains and grew to the size of cats. Lice too were a constant problem, bred through crowded unsanitary conditions. Inhabiting the seams of dirty uniforms, they caused ceaseless itching and repeated cycles of high fever accompanied by joint and muscle pain, rashes, and severe headache.

A debilitating kidney condition known as trench nephritis, incurred as a result of strep throat, plagued the soldiers. Trench foot, a wasting disease of the flesh, crippled many. It was the price of prolonged exposure to cold and wet conditions, the men's feet being bound up in puttees and boots for days on end. Left untreated, feet became gangrenous and required amputation. At the Front, the only solution was to change into clean dry socks as often as possible, and to grease the feet well with stinking whale oil (rendered from blubber of the right whale). Under conditions like the Somme and Passchendaele, a battalion of men used up to ten gallons of whale oil each day.

Gas gangrene, a potentially lethal bacterial infection, commonly developed from various *Clostridium* bacteria present in the chalky soils of northwestern France and especially in Flanders, where the clay-rich ground had been intensively farmed for generations. Those bacteria, well adapted to their natural harsh conditions, proliferated after being introduced, for example, via shrapnel wounds, into the new nutrient-rich environment of their human host. The non-hygienic surgical procedures at the Front did little to inhibit progress of the disease, which inevitably led to a buildup of lethal toxins and the discharge of putrid gas. Amputation was often the only solution to avoiding early death.

Less threatening to the front line foot soldier was trench mouth, a severe form of gingivitis, developed from a combination of stress, poor food, inadequate oral hygiene, and heavy smoking. The abundance of tobacco supplied by the army helped calm the nerves, suppressed appetites, and somewhat masked the stench of decaying bodies. But it took a toll. In worst-case scenarios the solution was removal of all teeth, and there were considerable numbers of toothless soldiers following the war. Titus was not among them. His dental certificate for demobilization shows that he required only five fillings before receiving a clean bill of health on May 6, 1919, in Bramshott, England.

Although he managed to keep his teeth for the duration of the war, Titus's dental fortunes ran out in the late 1930s after he developed severe gingivitis during a lengthy sea voyage. My sister Carolyn remembers it well. She had been playing doctor to our brother George and had cut off all his eyelashes with scissors. Titus, having just returned newly toothless from the dentist, was utterly outraged, but quite unable to speak. The best he could manage was to splutter, so splutter he did, and at great length. Such was his condition that he was at last compelled to write out to his young daughter the most severe penalty he could imagine: You will not be allowed to go to the exhibition. This was fall, when the Lunenburg County Fisheries Exhibition was, for country folk and especially for schoolchildren, one of the highlights of the year.

Titus rarely spoke of the horrors of trench warfare, but they were never far from the fathomless reservoir of his memory. One typical flashback occurred in the Harbourview Cemetery in Upper Rose Bay, where Titus would later be buried. In Rose Bay, family members regularly walked down to the shore where we kept a small boat. My brother George recalls once when, accompanied by Father, he was warned in no uncertain terms not to pick berries in the cemetery.

"No berries! No! No! You can't eat any of those berries! It's not right! Not from the cemetery! You shouldn't do that!" Titus tried to explain to his young son, remembering the grim realities of the killing fields of France and Flanders. His moral witness was not that of an innocent civilian. His eyes saw other things than a simple berry patch on a burial ground.

As an ordinary soldier he had endured week after week in the bowels of cemeteries, in fetid trenches surrounded by cadavers in various stages of decay. Time and again he had seen comrades killed, had helped in their burials at night, only to find them unearthed during some later bombardment. The dismembered and thoroughly mixed mortal remains of those unfortunate souls were in due course committed to mass graves, with belated blessings, like those at Essex Farm in Flanders Fields. For the sake of appearances, however, those grisly harvests are now properly marked by carefully spaced individual tombstones.

Trenches have been an integral part of warfare since time immemorial. In an earlier war the "Front" might have been ranks of spears and pikes. But, without question, it was only after the French and English combined forces to halt the initial German advance on Paris in early September 1914 that the trademark colossal wastage of humanity in trench warfare was born. Given the technology of the day and the shrinking space to maneuver, the conflict was concentrated between opposing lines of trenches.

On the Western Front the Great War was characterized by entrenchment warfare. The only exceptions applied to the initial phase of the war, pre-September 1914, and towards the end, following the breakthrough made by the Allies in August 1918. By the time the 85th Battalion arrived in the field in February 1917, defense systems consisting of numerous disconnected sections and irregular lines of trenches had been either dug out by hand or, more often because of boggy ground, built up of wood and sandbags. Systems of trenches extended as a double line across Europe along the entire 400-mile-long Front from Switzerland to the coast of northern France.

For the Allies, a main fire trench, typically with a parapet heightened and reinforced with sandbags, faced the enemy. Fifty to seventy yards behind this, a supporting trench four or five feet deep was in turn linked up with the reserve trench 800 to 1,000 yards distant, all of which were joined by communication trenches connecting a zigzag line. Dugouts, protective holes burrowed into the sides of trenches, were reserved for officers and senior NCOs (non-commissioned officers). Positioned about a thousand yards behind the reserve trench was the field artillery, and behind that, heavy artillery occupied camouflaged gun pits. German trench systems were even more complex, in many instances layered back to a distance measured in miles. Barbed wire entanglements were in some locations up to a hundred feet deep.

At Vimy Ridge, the German defensive trench system was backed by underground concrete shelters, and with wide belts of barbed wire and machine-gun emplacements. The four-mile-long ridge stood out as a veritable fortress.

The men slept where they could find a space and in wet weather sheltered beneath their groundsheets. Soldiers were in front line or support line trenches, six hours on, six hours off, for about eight days at a time. After this interval, with luck, their relief would arrive and they would rotate to the reserve trenches for four or five days. While duty in the reserve lines offered some ease, it was scarcely a holiday, for no matter front line or reserve, the men were liable for work details at any time. Trench repair was the most strenuous, but there were always dugouts to prepare, wiring parties to assist, and ammunition and supplies to carry to the front lines (which in some cases amounted to a slog of several miles under heavy loads and harassment by enemy fire), all in addition to gear cleaning, inspection and various drills. There was little respite.

Smoke from cooking generally drew enemy fire, so hot food had to be clumsily carried in "hay boxes," arriving late or sometimes not at all. The boxes were basically cookers in which food was heated to the boiling point, then insulated with hay and left to cook by the heat trapped in the container. The idea was to conserve rationed cooking oil. The Front on either side was under constant observation by snipers and lookouts. This required that crucial supply and maintenance be carried out at night when set procedures of supply, troop movements, repair work, wiring, and the activities of raiding parties went ahead. An hour before dawn came the "stand to," everyone being roused to man their positions and guard against a dawn raid.

Poet Wilfred Owen, a British lieutenant in the lines, described battle conditions under which he and fellow soldiers went ten days or more with little sleep, without washing, and without being able to take off their boots. Thus, battling the weather, the mud, the water, and the squalid conditions, as well as "Fritz," life on the firing line in trench warfare consisted of long intervals of excruciating discomfort and boredom broken abruptly by shocking shifts of abject terror.

In all this there was absolutely no privacy, and in consequence promiscuity and obscenity became a way of life. In *Sexual Life During the Great War,* Fischer and Dubois suggest that "the fact that the most intimate aspects of the individual's physiological life were public, and that disemboweled and otherwise mutilated corpses were a common sight, rendered decent language a matter of no importance, and it might even be said that civilized restraint in that direction would have been misplaced in such an environment."

6

Lead-up to Vimy

Siol Na Fear Fearail
(The Breed of Manly Men)

– *Motto of the 85th Battalion worn on the soldier's cap badge*

It was a long, desolate winter in Witley Camp. Cold and wet in overcrowded huts, the troops suffered from flu, enteritis and meningitis. Despite discourses and sermons on clean living, and "manly Christianity," venereal disease was widespread. Then, at departure time, 269 men of the battalion were left at Witley to recover from an epidemic of mumps. Those unfortunates would catch up later. Titus's childhood immunity exempted him from this particular plague. Already depleted to under 1,000 members, the 85th crossed the English Channel on February 10, 1917, although their joy on departure was seriously tempered by an exceedingly rough passage. Titus likely weathered the voyage from Folkstone to Le Havre better than most of his companions in arms, battened down as they were between decks on the SS *London*.

Ashore at last in France, the 85th Battalion boarded trains, heading north-northeast to Boulogne-sur-Mer. There they encamped for a couple of days, enjoying a brief acclimatization before heading for the Front. Finally, very early on the morning of February 13, the troops climbed into a long train of boxcars empty of seats, light, and heat, arriving at midnight in Houdain, about twelve miles west-northwest of Vimy.

It remained now for the troops and their support group of drivers, cooks, gunners, and medical officers to make their way further up the line. Even the hardy Canadians felt the cold, for the European winter of 1916-1917 was one of the coldest on record. The chronicles report that cold, stiff, and hungry after their trip in boxcars designed for "8 Cheveux, 40 Hommes," (8 horses, 40 men) they immediately set out on an eight-mile march to a forward camp near the front lines. The night was bitterly frigid, cloudless and starlit. Far in the northeast an intermittently flickering light became increasingly bright and insistent. A thunderous rumbling soon overcame the steady crunching rhythm of boots on frozen ground. The guns, at least, were not cold – the merciless, tireless, hot-roaring guns.

At this stage in its advance, the battalion consisted of 46 officers and 978 O.R. (other ranks), under its normal full strength of about 1,150 men. Reinforcements would not arrive until early March. Second in command to Lt. Col. Allison H. Borden was Lt. Col. Earle C. Phinney, with Major James L. Ralston as Adjutant. By this time, Canadian and Newfoundland troops had been fighting in France and in Flanders for two years. By the end of June 1915, the first three Canadian divisions had all been tested under fire in soul-searing engagements at Ypres. In the fall of 1916, compatriots of the 85th Battalion fought alongside French and English troops in the Battle of the Somme. The 85th would eventually replace the 73rd Battalion in the 12th Infantry Brigade, 4th Canadian Division, in France and Belgium after the Battle of Vimy Ridge.

En route to Vimy, 222568 Rifleman Mossman and his comrades looked in vain for signs of towns, but little evidence remained except for stones and bricks hidden in the road beneath a thin cover of snow. On February 16, 1917, with base camp established in the battered remains of the ancient Château de la Haie, Phinney introduced the first contingent of troops to life in the front line trenches. They first stopped at a Field Ambulance advanced dressing station, where ghastly casualties were arriving from nearby trenches on the slopes of Vimy Ridge. At this time, non-sterile field surgery was the first line of defense when dealing with projectile wounds. Amputation was often the norm as medics raced the clock to forestall the spread of infection. Antibiotics were not in widespread use, and the science of blood transfusions was in the development stage. Nor was there more than a faint appreciation of germ theory. Only a decade or so before the Great War, doctors were using rhubarb-based purgatives to combat rickets and treating a range of other diseases with leeches.

Onward then, to the front line trenches, some only forty yards distant from those in which the enemy crouched in wait. Imminent prospects of death and desolation enveloped everyone along the firing line, although opposing trenches were not normally within bomb-throwing distance. Here at Vimy Ridge, the 85th would receive their baptism. That much was clear. Although difficult to describe, the experience would never be forgotten. The unvarnished grim realities on display along the Western Front during the Great War far exceeded anything manufactured since to horrify the modern filmgoer.

In mid-February 1917, troops of the 85th Battalion confronting Vimy Ridge sensed that big plans were afoot. At the Front, visits among the ranks occurred from time to time, and news had a way of spreading to and through the fighting units. The men knew about Haig's "Big Push" on the Somme, and they recalled the breakup of the Canadian Brigade to feed reinforcements to depleted British units prior to the departure of the 85th Battalion to France. However, they realized who was in charge. Although directly controlled by Canadian officers, all four divisions of the Canadian Corps responded to orders coming down the line from the Supreme Commander-in-Chief of the BEF. And those orders brooked no refusal. The Canadian Corps was, after all, only one of several corps which formed an integral part of the British First Army. And throughout virtually the entire war, British Headquarters was responsible for the tactical deployment of Canadian troops in the Canadian Expeditionary Force.

For Canadian troops, less class-driven than their English counterparts, Haig exemplified the rigid mentality of a high command disconnected from front-line reality. However much they may have respected their own officers, many men in the 85th had a visceral dislike of Haig, referring to him as The Butcher of the Somme. Before long they would encounter firsthand the inflexible approach and trademark tactics of conflict resolution of their Supreme Commander-in-Chief. Titus certainly had no love for Haig. He shook his head whenever the name came up, muttering to the effect that "No one liked Haig. We never saw him. He kept well out of sight, far behind the lines."

The soldiers realized, and generally accepted, that their view was limited to events on the ground. But neither could Haig have full understanding, given his studied avoidance of the close-up battle conditions in this war. His official war record, displayed as a brass-plated *curriculum vitae* on a plaque in St. George's Memorial Church, Ypres (modern day Ieper), is most impressive: FIELD MARSHAL SIR DOUGLAS HAIG (1861-1928), 1ST EARL HAIG OF BEMERSYDE, KT, GCB, OM, GCVO, KCIE COMMANDER I CORPS 1914, COMMANDER FIRST ARMY 1915, COMMANDER-IN-CHIEF BRITISH EXPEDITIONARY FORCE 1915-1919, FOUNDER OF THE ROYAL BRITISH LEGION.

Some influential authorities in the system (Winston Churchill among them) remained convinced that he had done well and thoroughly deserved his position as Commander-in-Chief. His title as First Earl Haig was approved by both houses of parliament and conferred by King George V in March 1919. Along with the title, Earl Haig was granted £100,000 to help him maintain the lifestyle of a Peer of the Realm. In fact he had asked for £250,000. Douglas Haig was used to money, having enjoyed financial independence since his youth as the son of a famous Scottish whisky distiller.

For contrast, take Lt. General Sir Julian H.G. Byng, Commander of the Canadian Corps at Vimy. Unusual for a British officer, Byng was no stuffed shirt. Nor was he a so-called Château General, far removed from the front lines. Both he and his senior commander, Major General Arthur W. Currie, were all over the Front at Vimy, maintaining uncharacteristically close communication with the troops. Special attention was given to making certain that all section leaders received maps, and that all officers – senior and non-commissioned officers alike – were informed of plans so they could take over in a worst-case scenario. To this end, Byng had thousands of topographic maps made and distributed to his officers. Currie supervised the implementation of all tactical details. Both men insisted on strict analysis and thorough preparation.

All this departed significantly from the practice in British armies, in which even junior officers were seldom told what a particular attack was intended to achieve. Seen to trust and respect their men, both senior officers were, in turn, respected and admired by soldiers of the 85th Battalion. Postwar, Titus unfailingly praised his Canadian commanding officers. Currie was especially well respected by the 85th because the men felt he stood up to the British and would not squander their lives. It was with great pride that Titus recalled Currie's constant presence in the line, instructing and encouraging officers and privates alike.

Currie, like many Canadian officers, was relatively unschooled. As Pierre Berton remarks in *Vimy*, "Here was a remarkable figure … without professional military experience, Currie had risen to major-general in less than three years and would soon climb up another notch in the military hierarchy. With only a high school education and a third-class teacher's certificate, he would be propelled after the war into the principalship of Canada's most famous university, McGill." Yet Currie's was the all-important common touch. He knew all his NCOs by name.

British High Command informed Byng the Canadians would play the central role in the planned spring 1917 offensive. As part of that offensive, Vimy Ridge had to be taken. It would prove a memorable triumph, and Currie was the recognized architect. For the first time in the war, all four Canadian divisions would fight together under command of the Canadian Corps. After Vimy Ridge, Currie would take over from Byng as commanding officer of all four divisions of the Canadian Corps.

Meanwhile, the search for mobility and hopes of a possible breakthrough continued on both sides. The Industrial Revolution was already over a century old and the wheels of change were turning ever more quickly. Machines were close to ruling men in this all-consuming industrial warfare. Great War weaponry, in addition to battleships, submarines, tanks and aircraft, included aerial bombing and machine-gun strafing, nests of light and heavy machine guns, poison gas, grenades, mortars and artillery, rifles, bayonets, booby traps, flame throwers, knives, pistols, and, in the close confines of the trenches, folding spades (trench-digging tools) and homemade clubs. Across this spectrum, artillery accounted for most casualties (an estimated 60 percent of military fatalities), especially head injuries due to exploding shells and fragmentation.

Strong ties to tradition in both British and German armies in some respects slowed their adoption of fresh techniques. For example, with the Germans, their hesitation in developing tanks would prove a costly error. For the BEF, dismissing the machine gun as overrated was good reason for the old stereotype of "lions led by donkeys." At the outset of the war both sides hauled field artillery into position at a gallop, and fired over open sights and only at what could be seen. However, as Hew Strachan states in *The First World War*, "The western front was an intensely competitive environment, where the innovation of one side was emulated, improved upon or negated by the other. Ironically, it was this very cycle of action and reaction, designed to break the deadlock, which confirmed it."

The problem of silencing the enemy guns long remained the generally recognized precondition for success. Then, for the BEF, the solution came about through the meeting of several exceptionally capable minds willing to work on developing scientific gunnery. In this, General Byng's choice of Andrew McNaughton as Counter Battery Staff Officer for the Canadian Corps proved crucial. An engineer by training, McNaughton was quick to assemble his team during the lead-up to Vimy. With full support from Lt. General Currie, himself a former militia gunnery officer, improvements continued to be made in developing a counter-battery system to protect the infantry.

McNaughton's team explored several options to pinpoint enemy artillery, including "sound-ranging" and "flash-spotting." Flash-spotting, a technique requiring visually accurate triangulation of a muzzle flash, was viewed with skepticism in the British Third Army; sound-ranging was not even considered possible, although the French had begun similar studies in mid-1915. For MacNaughton, effective counter-battery analysis and reply in kind to the enemy's destructive sound and light show called for absolutely precise triangulation.

The key player on McNaughton's team was Lieutenant Lawrence Bragg, who, at twenty-seven, was already a Nobel Laureate in physics. They would focus their research on sound-ranging, the principles of which were directly analogous to Bragg's particular expertise, namely, the behaviour of "reflections" of chemical structures from X-radiation. Specifically, sound-ranging relied on an array of microphones to record the point of origin of low-frequency sound waves from a firing gun. Unlike flash-ranging, it worked under conditions of poor visibility to provide cross bearings to locate the source of artillery fire. In terms of distances and angles, it all boiled down to an elegant exercise in high school geometry. The system of sound-ranging was well advanced by Vimy. Further improvements made during The Hundred Days Offensive late in the war would bring the technique close to perfection and gain wide recognition for the artillery as the Great War winner.

The lowly foot soldiers of the Canadian Corps, though possibly unaware of the work of MacNaughton's team, were thoroughly familiar with the various weapons available to them. Titus and his comrades relied first and foremost on the .303 Lee-Enfield. Adopted as standard for the foot soldier early in the war, it replaced the Ross, a Canadian-made .303 army rifle. The Ross was basically a target rifle, which proved far too delicate to function well (except for snipers) under conditions on the Western Front. The Lee-Enfield survived to see service in the Second World War. It held ten cartridges, outperforming the German Mauser, which held only five. Mills bombs, grenades the size of tennis balls, were lobbed either by hand or as a rifle grenade propelled by a blank cartridge. Mills bombs and the Lewis light machine gun were counted among the soldier's greatest assets.

At twenty-eight pounds, the Lewis light machine gun was very popular among the Canadians. Although carried and operated by a single soldier, a helper was useful to carry and load the 47-round ammo drums. These drums could be dispensed in either one five-second blast or short bursts of five rounds each. Invented by an American, the Lewis gun was initially manufactured in Belgium and then adapted to fire British ammo. It proved extremely useful and won the respect of the Germans, who referred to it as "the Belgian rattlesnake." Their own top-quality light machine gun, the MG08, fired 600 rounds per minute.

Twice the weight of the Lewis, the Vickers heavy machine gun was a tremendously durable workhorse for the Allies. Operated by a three-man crew, it fired from a tripod and was water-cooled. Ammo was fed in 250-round belts which lasted thirty seconds at 500 shots per minute. Unfortunately, it was late in the war before it was discovered that the heavy and cumbersome water-cooling apparatus was not absolutely essential for operation.

Totally counter to General Haig's fixed opinions, machine guns proved to be extremely destructive weapons. Although the prototype had appeared during the American Civil War, the new models were far more deadly. As things turned out, the Canadians were better outfitted with machine guns than the British for much of the Great War. However, it took time to convince Haig about the truth of the matter.

At Vimy Ridge the Canadians employed machine guns in "creeping barrages," in combination with artillery fire, with machine gun bullets falling ahead of the artillery shells to catch retreating infantry and to impede possible enemy counterattack. The technique, known as "indirect fire," delivered destruction at an invisible target.

My father recalled that day and night, week after week, dozens of machine guns were kept firing toward distant positions where the enemy was known to be concentrated. This strategy was invented and put into practice as early as 1915 by Raymond Brutinel, a French army reserve officer serving with the 1st Canadian Machine Gun Brigade. A much decorated individual, General Brutinel was Corps Machine Gun Officer from late 1916 to the end of the war. Under ideal conditions, the result of indirect machine-gun fire was akin to that achieved by English longbows at Agincourt on Saint Crispin's Day in 1415.

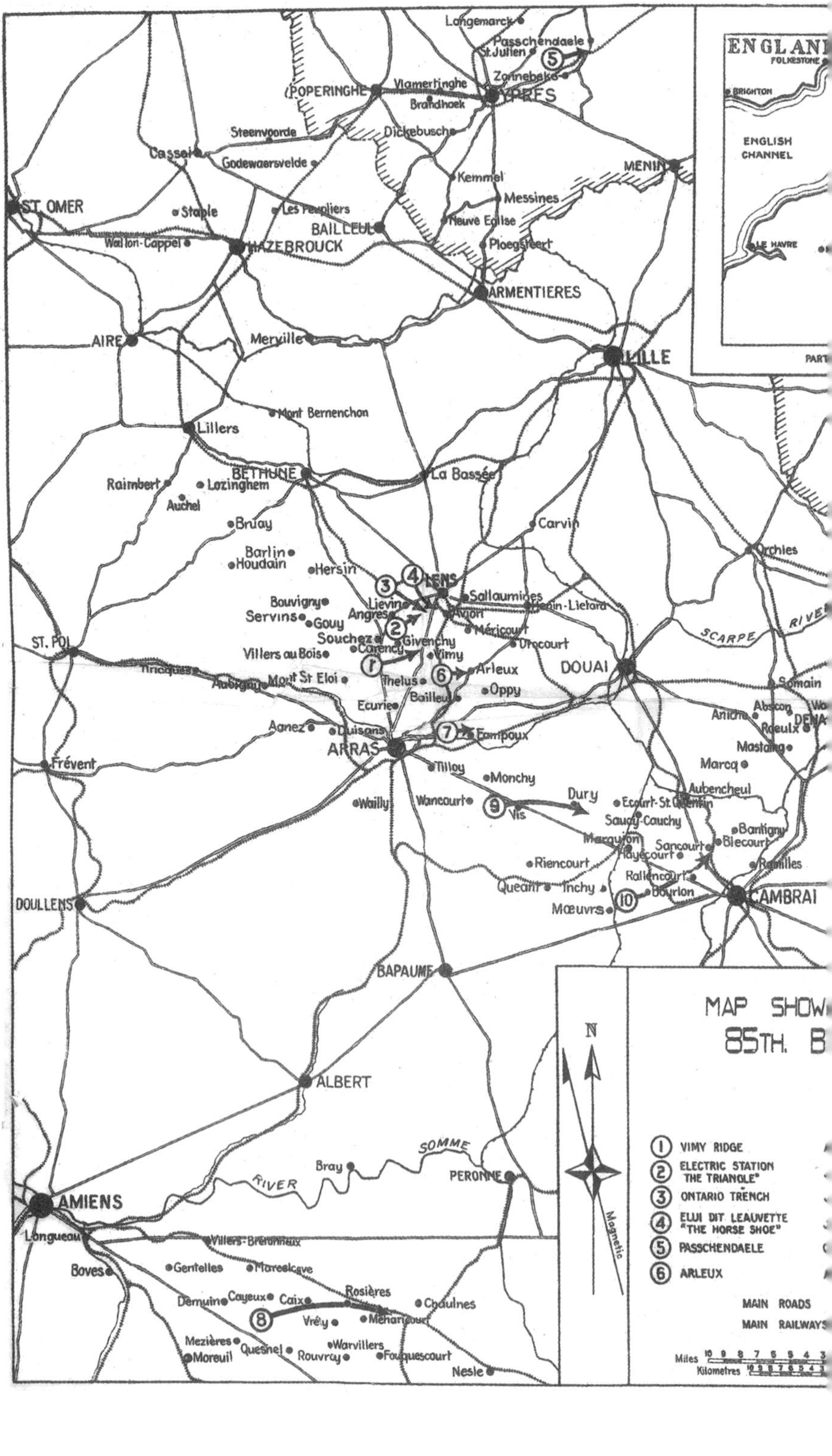
ENGLAND
FOLKESTONE
BRIGHTON
ENGLISH CHANNEL
LE HAVRE
Langemarck
Passchendaele
St.Julien
Zonnebeke
POPERINGHE
Vlamertinghe
Brandhoek
YPRES
Steenvoorde
Dickebusch
Cassel
Godewaersvelde
Kemmel
MENIN
Messines
ST. OMER
Staple
Les Peupliers
BAILLEUL
Neuve Eglise
Wallon-Cappel
HAZEBROUCK
Ploegsteert
ARMENTIERES
AIRE
Merville
LILLE
Mont Bernenchon
Lillers
BETHUNE
La Bassée
Raimbert
Lozinghem
Auchel
Bruay
Carvin
Barlin
Houdain
Hersin
Orchies
LENS
Sallaumines
Lievin
Henin-Lietard
Bouvigny
Angres
Avion
Servins
Gouy
Méricourt
Souchez
Givenchy
Drocourt
Carency
SCARPE RIVER
Villers au Bois
Vimy
ST. POL
Arleux
DOUAI
Tincques
Aubigny
Mont St Eloi
Thelus
Oppy
Somain
Bailleul
Ecurie
Abscon
Agnez
Duisans
Fampoux
Roeulx
ARRAS
Mastaing
Frévent
Tilloy
Marcq
Monchy
Aubencheul
Wailly
Wancourt
Dury
Ecourt-St.Quentin
Vis
Saudy-Cauchy
Bantigny
Marquion
Sancourt
Blecourt
Haynecourt
Riencourt
Ramilles
Raillencourt
Queant
Inchy
Bourlon
DOULLENS
Mœuvres
CAMBRAI
BAPAUME
MAP
85TH.
N
Magnetic
ALBERT
SOMME
RIVER
Bray
PERONNE
AMIENS
Longueau
Villers-Bretonneux
Boves
Gentelles
Marcelcave
Rosières
Demuin
Cayeux
Caix
Chaulnes
Vrély
Méharicourt
Mezières
Warvillers
Moreuil
Quesnel
Rouvroy
Fouquescourt
Nesle
1 VIMY RIDGE
2 ELECTRIC STATION "THE TRIANGLE"
3 ONTARIO TRENCH
4 ELUI DIT LEAUVETTE "THE HORSE SHOE"
5 PASSCHENDAELE
6 ARLEUX
MAIN ROADS
MAIN RAILWAYS
Miles
Kilometres

A map of France and Flanders, from Titus's archives, showing some of the battles the 85th Battalion, Nova Scotia Highlanders, participated in:

(1) Vimy Ridge, April 9-14, 1917.

(2) Electric Station, "The Triangle" June 20, 1917.

(3) Ontario Trench, June 26, 1917.

(4) Eleu dit Leauvette, Avion Horse Shoe June 28, 1917.

(5) Passchendaele, October 28-31, 1917.

(6) Arleux, April 16-May 6, 1918.

(7) Fampoux, July 24-31, 1918.

(8) Amiens, August 8-10, 1918.

(9) Arras-Mt. Dury, Drocourt-Quéant Line September 1918.

(10) Cambrai, September 27-October 1, 1918.

(11) Valenciennes, Mons, October 23-November 2, 1918.

(12) Quievrechain, November 6, 1918.

7

Hallowed Ground

We stand on hallowed ground. A place of agonized conflict, a site of appalling loss of life, a vessel of sorrow, a crucible of courage, a hallmark of ingenuity, collaboration and resolve undertaken by men at arms in the cause of peace.

– Gov. Gen. David Johnston
at Vimy Ridge Memorial,
April 9, 2012

The Germans were especially well-equipped with mortar bombs of various sizes (from "piss tins" to "rum jars" in soldier's jargon). The *Minenwerfer* (flying mine) was the most powerful. Unlike a rifle bullet, which travels in a nearly straight line faster than sound, the noise made by a "Moaning Minnie" reached the target before the projectile. The launch of a large Minnie, up to three and a half feet in length, was heralded by a moaning sound as it wobbled its way along a high arc towards its target. The largest *Minenwerfer* was filled with scrap iron and nearly two hundred pounds of high explosives, linked to a short fuse. Shrapnel, the shards of jagged metal from the exploding shells of mortars and artillery, is thought to have caused most casualties on the battlefield during the Great War. Reportedly, Moaning Minnies could kill by concussion alone, presumably by the destruction of internal organs, a conclusion reached after finding physically unmarked dead close beside craters produced by exploding Minnies.

Of all weapons brought to bear upon the Allied forces, Titus feared the Moaning Minnies most of all. His introduction to the devastating blasts of these mortar shells occurred at Vimy. This I learned during one of our annual homegrown New Year's Eve celebrations.

New Year's Eve was always a big event at home, measured by the number of *Belsnickles* (Lunenburg County's equivalent of Newfoundland mummers) who turned up at the door. The practice used to be enthusiastically carried out from Christmas through New Year's Eve, and a good deal of effort went into searching out an effective disguise. By the early 1950s, the advent of television in country homes pretty much brought this ancient custom to an end. However, Titus always believed in bringing in the New Year with a bang. Without fail he would load up around midnight, step outside no matter the weather, and fire off a couple of blasts with his single-barrelled shotgun. Although firing the old year out was a well-established custom in Lunenburg County, it doubtless had added value for him, seeing as it coincided with his birthday.

One year he suggested to me we could set off a really big blast to use up a pound or so of old black powder he kept on hand to load his own ammunition. A twelve-year-old, I was of course quick to agree. Normally, making a homemade bomb would be a challenging undercover job. To have parental initiative for such a project was unheard of. Noting my mother's apprehension, Father quickly explained we'd play it safe and set things up down on the shore.

So, off we went, loaded down with bomb-making material, shortly before midnight. I'd heard my father talk about

Moaning Minnies and speculated whether the blast would be anything like the one a Minnie would make.

"I doubt it," he replies skeptically, "but it ought to make a fair bit of a racket." Then, warming to the subject, he adds, "There were a lot o' Minnies fired off at Vimy. They were shot from huge trench mortars, kind o' like artillery, except they were fired from huge muzzle-loaders aimed high in the air. That way, they could drop right down on top of you. Wasn't much you could do about it, except maybe pray."

"Did you pray much?"

"There were times that I did, but day or night, it didn't really matter much, you could see 'em comin', just like giant firecrackers, trailin' sparks an' moanin' low, kind o' like a ghost. *Wooo! Wooo! Wooo!* A feller's hair would stand right up on end, an' you hadn't much time. You had to figure out pretty fast whereabouts it was headed."

"Why was that?" I ask, out of pure ignorance.

"Well, this was a big heavy front line gun, except I t'ink some of 'em were rifled. And Fritz generally angled 'em to shoot high. They come in a couple o' different sizes. But no matter what, if a Minnie was headed your way an' caught you in the open, best t'ing to do was to flatten yourself on the ground. At times like that, the ground was your friend – get as low as you could in the mud, dirt, water, no matter what – an' quick about it, as far from the landin' point as you could manage before it hit."

Our makeshift Moaning Minnie, set up near the high tide mark, consisted of several cans of black powder, covered with a galvanized bucket and weighted down with a large rock. Everything was going according to plan, I reckoned. Getting a head start on the celebration, a few distant shotgun blasts sounded like firecrackers. Father lit the fuse, and the two bombardiers scuttled for safety behind some nearby scrub spruce. I led the charge into a camouflaged blind that I used to hunt black ducks. On the shore below Harbourview Cemetery, zero hour, according to our timing, rang in with a resounding *Whump!* Not quite the tremendous blast I had been expecting, but nevertheless a respectable racket.

Unfortunately, there was little evidence of a crater, and although the bucket bore some impressive dents, there was no sign of shrapnel wounds. True to the Moaning Minnies legend, there was a most gratifying shower of sparks. But it was just as well that the BEF did not have to rely upon Titus to supply innovations in weaponry.

On the Somme, neither shrapnel nor high explosives could destroy the German barbed wire. Tragically, the hand-held British wire cutters supplied to the struggling soldiers failed their intended task. High explosives could do the job, but only if the explosion was precisely timed to go off upon impact with the wire. Success was achieved, at last, with the introduction of the No. 106 "instantaneous fuse" at Vimy in April 1917. This enabled artillery shells to explode upon impact with barbed wire and destroy it through a splintering effect.

By this time, early spring 1917, the blood-soaked slopes of Vimy Ridge had been fought over for more than two years. Kaiser Billy's boys, well-practiced by now, maintained superb observation over the terrain and a constant harassing fire. Soldiers on both sides were well acquainted with death's many faces, the torment of lice and rats, trench foot, the stench of latrines, of bodies long unburied, and repeated gut-wrenching moments of truth when going over.

Three British armies were committed to a broad frontal assault on the Germans during this phase of the so-called Second Battle of Arras. After five months of elaborate preparations, the curtain was set to rise on the opening show in the Battle of Vimy Ridge. On the north end of the line, the Canadian Corps of the First Army was ready. This would be the first major engagement for the 85th Nova Scotia Highlanders. Beside them, to the south and in the centre, the Third Army would attack from Arras. On their right flank, the Fifth Army would attack on the south end of the line.

The overall objective of the British forces was to achieve a breakthrough and thus end the war.

On Vimy's western slopes, the Allied forces eagerly awaited zero hour. Up until 1916, unarmed pipers always led the Highland regiments ("devils in skirts" to the Germans) over the top. More than 500 pipers were killed in the Great War and over twice that number wounded. The difficulty of replacing them led to a change heartily welcomed by pipers everywhere – at Vimy Ridge the skirl of the pipes issued from behind the line of trenches where, during the initial charge, pipers kept company with stretcher bearers. In this way the unconscionably high attrition rate of qualified pipers was much reduced. To this day, musicians in the Ceremonial Guard wear epaulettes as a symbol of their one-time association with, and indeed their secondary role as, stretcher bearers. By way of trivia, and for some curious reason, the kilts and accoutrements for proper Highland dress had not been forwarded to the 85th Battalion from Scotland. Chances are that wearing apparel was, at this point, not quite the battalion's most important concern.

Zero hour was set for the morning of Easter Monday, April 9, 1917, at 5:30 a.m. The idea was that this would prove important timing from the aspect of religious symbolism, given the character of the anticipated sacrifice. Jack Sheldon, in *The German Army at Vimy Ridge 1914-1917*, describes the event from the German perspective:

When the day dawned, wet and cold, at 5.30 a.m. on 9 April, a storm of fire, unparalleled in anyone's experience, crashed down over the German positions. Its impacts were like the deafening roar and tossing of a sea lashed by a hurricane. Everywhere great fountains of earth rose in the air. The earth seemed to quake. Whilst the front line was engaged primarily with light guns and mortars, supported by massed machine guns, the support lines and battery positions came under fire from medium, heavy and super heavy guns, as well as being drenched with gas. The fumes and smoke which hung over the German positions grew into dark masses of cloud, which glowed red. All the roads which the reserves moving forward would need to use were lashed by fire. Yellow flares rose all along the German lines, but before the defending batteries could bring down defensive fire, the hail of fire lifted from the front lines, only to fall with increased violence on the depth positions. Even the curtains of machine gun fire, which had been raking the German front line parapets, permitting the sentries only to observe by the use of periscopes, lifted. In many places the earth itself opened up as mines and subway exits were blown.

Audible in England, the intense preliminary barrage went on non-stop for an hour and forty minutes. Simultaneously, thousands of cannons crashed out with a barely perceptible lapse at brief intervals, signalling the slight successive elevation of the guns. The well-designed BEF recipe for the so-called rolling or creeping barrage swept the German lines front to back in roughly fifty-yard advancing increments. Six million shells, on average 1,000 per second, were delivered. The Germans, of course, had their own recipes for a creeping barrage, or *Glocke*, as they called it, but to this calculated firestorm their reply was muted. MacNaughton's counter-battery work helped to ensure this result by destroying an estimated 70 percent of the enemy guns before the battle began.

The four Canadian divisions advanced steadily until seriously checked at Hill 145. This promontory was the pivot point on Vimy Ridge which, at this crucial point in the battle, continued to anchor the sagging German line.

In the lead-up to Vimy, the 85th Battalion had been assigned the role of support group. Their *War Diary*, which records their day-to-day activities, states that for several weeks prior to zero hour, the battalion was occupied in constructing and filling ammunition dumps, digging a deep dugout and connecting trenches, carrying barbed wire, lugging ammunition to forward positions, escorting prisoners of war, and serving as prisoner of war (POW) guards. A and B companies were seconded to the 47th Battalion from British Columbia.

Kilts or no kilts, three days into the battle, the 85th Battalion stood out as the least decimated of the 4th Division. In consequence, Brigade HQ called upon them to prepare to assault Hill 145. This highest point on Vimy Ridge was a formidable redoubt, honeycombed with concrete dugouts and networks of machine-gun posts. Commanding Officer Lt. Col. A.H. Borden selected C and D companies, led by Captain Percival Anderson of Cape Breton, for the honour of taking Hill 145. Initially A and B companies would stolidly maintain their essentially non-combat role among many supporting groups in this great endeavour.

For some unknown reason that day, the usual barrage preliminary to going over the top did not materialize at the appointed time. Nevertheless, despite the lack of supporting fire, C and D companies went over in the midst of a snowstorm, and by the morning of April 10 had basically accomplished their objective. The *War Diary* tersely reports on the successful action as follows:

The Company Commanders were on the outward flanks of their Companies, and owing to the winding nature of the new front line trench were out of sight. The C.O. decided [it] was folly to attempt, at Zero hour, to alter the plan. He feared that it might result in disconcerted action, as it was impossible to communicate any further orders to everyone concerned before Zero hour. He waited to see whether the Companies would advance without a barrage.

A half minute after Zero C Company on the left moved calmly and deliberately out of the trenches, the advance was taken up by D Coy. In spite of Machine Gun and rifle fire from the enemy, which immediately opened, the attack was pressed home, the Companies providing their own covering fire by Lewis Guns firing from the hip and riflemen firing on the move.

Many of the Germans, finding it impossible to stop the advance turned and ran, but were soon put out of action by our fire. About 20 prisoners, including 3 officers were taken, 2 Hun officers and about 70 other ranks were killed. At least 3 machine guns were captured.

With respect to Titus's involvement in this particular operation, A and B companies only caught up with their sister companies on April 10, in time to contribute to the business of mopping up. Such operations doubtless held their own particular hazards. By April 14, 1917, the battle was over. Ten days after that, Titus wore two stripes of a corporal on his shoulder as he laboured with comrades constructing roads over Vimy Ridge so supplies and artillery could be brought up to the Front.

As a postscript to this brief account of the Canadian Corps victory, it is worth noting that, according to Jack Sheldon, a noted authority on the German military of World War I, German Army records reveal they did not consider they had been defeated at Vimy. They attributed their failure to repel the British forces to a lack of adequate reserves and inadequate artillery support. Their view was that no massive breakthrough had occurred and very little vital ground had been lost. Crucial to their aim, they continued to hold the Douai Plain and its coal deposits to the east of Vimy Ridge; these fossil fuel deposits helped power the industrial giant Krupp, who produced their armaments.

Overall, the Second Battle of Arras failed to achieve the intended breakthrough. Of the three armies, only the Canadian Corps reached their objective to capture Vimy Ridge. Thus, the Battle of Vimy Ridge, and Canada's central role in it, stood out as a harbinger of hope for the Allies. Through it all, the four Canadian divisions worked efficiently as one to achieve the nation-building victory. The tribute went to Currie as strategist, for which he was promoted to Lieutenant General and knighted on June 4, 1917, by

King George V in George's Birthday Honours. General Julian Byng, Currie's superior officer, was promoted to General in Command of the British Third Army. Later bestowed the title Lord Byng of Vimy, he survived to serve as Governor General of Canada from 1921 to 1926.

Vimy Ridge remained in Allied hands for the duration of the war. As for the butcher's bill, the 85th Battalion lost 56 killed and 282 wounded, many of whom died later of their wounds. Total casualties amounted to over 25 percent of battalion strength. Total Canadian Corps casualties, according to Nicholson in his monumental *Canadian Expeditionary Force 1914-1919*, were 10,602 all ranks over the six-day action (April 9-14) – 3,598 of them fatal.

At the top of Hill 145 the Vimy Memorial stands in commemoration of great loss and the grief of war. Two huge soaring pylons representing France and Canada consist of steel-reinforced concrete frames to which is bonded fine quality light grey limestone blocks won from the Seget quarry near Split in Croatia. This quarry also supplied the stone for Roman Emperor Diocletian's palace in the third century AD. The inscription at the base of the Vimy Ridge Memorial reads: TO THE VALOUR OF THEIR COUNTRYMEN IN THE GREAT WAR AND IN MEMORY OF THEIR SIXTY THOUSAND DEAD THIS MONUMENT IS RAISED BY THE PEOPLE OF CANADA.

After Vimy, the need for replacements became painfully obvious to the warlords. The call came to Canadians on July 6, 1917, as the Military Services Act was passed and became law on December 26, 1917. This translated to the conscription of 56,000 more Canadian troops before war's end. By November 11, 1918, Canada had sent half a million soldiers overseas. Personal income tax was implemented at this time as a temporary measure, of course, to help defray costs. Practically every regiment raised in Canada on behalf of Great Britain and her global dominions had a contingent of so-called "Bluenose boys."

8

Lead-up to Passchendaele

It is like the eternal place of gnashing of teeth; the Slough of Despond could be contained in one of its crater-holes; the fires of Sodom and Gomorrah could not light a candle to it – to find the way to Babylon the Fallen. It is pock-marked like a body of foulest disease, and its odour is the breath of cancer. I have not seen any dead. I have done worse. In the dank air I have perceived it, and in the darkness, felt.

– Lt. Wilfred Owen[1]
January 19, 1917

Titus did not speak much about the Battle of Vimy Ridge. Nor, for reasons which may shortly become clear, did he ever even mention Passchendaele. I was never able to persuade him to accept an invitation for us to play tourist and visit the old battlegrounds in France and Flanders.

1 Lieutenant Wilfred Owen (1893-1918), 2nd Manchesters, in a letter to his mother written on the Western Front. Owen was killed November 4, 1918, seven days before the armistice.

Curiously, he did voice surprising enthusiasm for volunteering in raiding parties and scouting missions. Trench raids were initiated by the Canadians early in 1915. Generally, the weapons of choice were light and easy to use: clubs, knives, picks, shovels, Mills bombs, and revolvers. The objective of a trench raid was to secure prisoners as a source of intelligence about the enemy. At first they involved hundreds of men. However, the element of surprise was difficult to achieve under such conditions and several major disasters occurred, including one on the slopes of Hill 145 several weeks before the battle. When Currie took over as Commander-in-Chief of Canadian Corps following Vimy, he greatly reduced the number of men committed to trench raids. Correspondingly, the success rate went up, as did the amount of information gained.

Quite apart from the details concerning possible capture of a prisoner, raids had several dark sides. To hear Titus tell it: "You'd be out there in No Man's Land, makin' your way, crawlin' as often as not, best you could, lookin' for a way through the wire. Then suddenly, there'd be a sound like a tire goin' flat underneath your hand or under a man's body. *Fizzz!* An' an awful smell too. But you soon got used to it. You didn't worry about 'em. It was the live ones you had to worry about. Then a flare would go up, an' you'd see the rats, all red-eyed, scurryin' around. Flares didn't bother 'em none."

In raiding, Canadians were not only expert on offense, but are believed to have excelled at defense too. The *Home-Coming Programme* (dated June 9, 1919) for the 85th Battalion notes the exceptional fact that the Germans only took one prisoner from the 85th Battalion during the entire war. Records confirm that taking prisoners was no simple matter, for some officers on each side had an avowed policy of not taking any. Furthermore, prisoners were prone to fatal "accidents" when crossing No Man's Land, never more so than when their captors were Canadian.

In *Goodbye to All That*, Robert Graves writes,

Nearly every instructor in the mess could quote specific instances of prisoners having been murdered on the way back. The commonest motives were, it seems, revenge for the death of friends or relatives, jealousy of the prisoner's trip to a comfortable prison camp in England, military enthusiasm, fear of being suddenly overpowered by the prisoners or, more simply, impatience with the escorting job. The troops that had the worst reputation for acts of violence against prisoners were the Canadians ...

The front lines held special hazards for officers too.

My brother George recalls one occasion as a boy when he heard our father holding forth passionately on the subject of "fragging" to several former comrades. The old soldier told his friends that although he knew it happened, he did not approve of the practice. Ignoring his young son, Titus reminded his adult listeners that killing an officer while going over provided an ideal solution for anyone wanting to get rid of an unpopular leader. His concern was well justified because although the targets of fragging were usually officers perceived as reckless or incompetent, even a competent but strict commanding officer – or an NCO, like Sergeant Mossman – could become a target.

The weapon of choice that gives the name to this brand of so-called friendly fire was usually a grenade, which fragments completely on explosion, leaving no traceable ballistic evidence. Titus might have added that raids were rich opportunities for fragging. Although there were doubtless many casualties of fragging on the Western Front during the Great War, the number is believed nowhere close to that of some later conflicts, particularly Vietnam.

In a trench raid, typically two or more volunteers set out at night to reconnoiter the No Man's Land between opposing trenches. This required the raiders to remain stock-still should the enemy suddenly launch Very lights (also known as star shells or flares) to illuminate their field of fire. At such moments the slightest movement might reveal the position of the raiders, resulting in hair-trigger action by vigilant machine gunners.

A successful trench raid might end in the killing or – better – capture of one or more enemy soldiers, and/or the disruption of a section of enemy trenches. The capture of an enemy could provide information on their troop disposition, numbers and movements. Raiding also kept the men awake, keen, and stimulated during what could be a dull, mind-numbing night shift. For the brave volunteers, taking a prisoner might even result in the grant of a day or two leave, though Titus never mentioned this specifically.

Years later he confided simply and nonchalantly that he (and I quote) "used to like going out on raids." Given that troops spent 60 to 70 percent of their time in the front line, or in support thereof, it may have been preferable to be raiding than rotting in mind-numbing boredom in the filthy confines of a trench. However, the transformation of a humble fisherman to volunteer for near suicidal missions pays tribute to the military's efficiency in establishing esprit de corps. After all, 222568 Rifleman Mossman, like most of his comrades, joined the 85th of his own free will. As Will R. Bird states in his remarkable book *Ghosts Have Warm Hands*, "The war changed men mightily."

One imagines that Titus's fluency in German would have been especially valuable on a scouting team. As far as I am aware, no one in his family ever thought to question him specifically on this point. However, he made it perfectly clear to me that he did converse in German with captured prisoners on occasion.

At the Front, advancement came quickly to men with leadership potential. The loss among junior officers and NCOs was more than twice as high as that from other ranks. Made Acting Sergeant on June 16, 1917, Titus was confirmed to the rank three months later. No longer just following orders, he was now being called upon to deliver a few of his own.

During the lead-up to Passchendaele, there was a series of bitterly contested engagements just south of Lens. These included Eleu dit Leauvette and Horse Shoe Trench, respectively on June 27 and June 28, 1917. It was at Horse Shoe Trench, between Avion and Eleu dit Leauvette, that Titus's best friend Billy was lost, an event that probably took some of the shine off any pride of promotion he may have experienced up to that point. Billy was one of four men named William in Titus's platoon No. 7. He was most likely Private William E. Harris of New Ross, the only William numbered in the *War Diary* among the twenty-eight fatalities incurred by the 85th during the engagement. Unfortunately, there is no photograph of Harris in Lt. Col. A.H. Borden's valuable document *A Short History and Photographic Record of the Nova Scotia Overseas Highland Brigade C.E.F.*

He told the story simply enough, though hesitatingly.

"Billy was one o' my very best friends. It was at the Horse Shoe, right by the Souchez River. We was piped over the top, just like usual. We had gone over t'ree times in two days, you. You got to hand it to the boys. Back and forth acrost No Man's Land, attack, retreat, an' then counterattack. It was kill or be killed. We was like wild animals then. Only later when it was over could we loaf about in the rear, an' play the fool.

"But all hell had broken loose. It was late afternoon an' we was pushin' on under cover of our artillery. I remember Billy runnin' along just ahead a bit an' off to one side when, just like that, I seen the top of his head peel off right above his eyes. Funny, but it was just like in slow motion, you. Billy, he just kept right on runnin' for a couple of steps, his blood an' brains flyin' all over. There was no stoppin' to help. But it was a hard t'ing to see him like that. What could a man do? It was shrapnel that did it. There was no shortage of that. Come out of nowhere."

Billy's fatal passing-out parade was recorded as a sort of movie in the mind of his best buddy. Titus was haunted by the question of why, of all people, his life was spared. Moreover, through his recent promotions he was, at this point, one of the officers blowing the whistle – a strident shriek commanding men over the top. Failure to respond to the summons meant severe punishment or even execution by firing squad. In this role he bore responsibility in sending men like Billy to their deaths.

Trench warfare held many private terrors. There are only so many bullets in the clip of the bolt-action .303 Lee-Enfield. Supposing a man was able to snap off a shot or two during his slogging run through the storm of metal, poison gas, and barbed wire entanglements, then the hand-to-hand fighting might begin. Brutally exhausting work, there was no alternative to execution by cold steel of either you or the enemy during the heat of close combat. Crazed brute instinct takes over and there is no question of practice making perfect.

Titus's archives include an unofficial photograph of him receiving instruction in bayonet fighting shortly after the 85th had been mobilized in 1916 at Aldershot in the Annapolis Valley (page 97). The bayonets are seventeen inches of regulation steel; they're never rubber, except perhaps in stage plays. Who took the photo, and why, will never be known. The time is high summer and it's evidently a warm day, judging by the "cow's breakfast" straw hats worn by the contestants at practice for the real thing. The instructor stands by, displaying a practiced casual attitude, clearly accepting that duels to the death of this sort would shortly be routine in the life of this breed of manly men.

In bayonet work, the primary target is the centre of the body. Few men with centre body wounds ever made it back alive to casualty stations. Bayonets fixed, men struggle up and over the top of their trench, to try to cross No Man's Land in the face of a murderous hail of gunfire. Ideally, according to the training procedures (and accompanied by copious

Bayonet practice in Platoon No. 7 at Camp Aldershot, Annapolis Valley, midsummer 1916. Titus is on the left, in the centre is an unidentified man – perhaps an instructor – and Frank L. Hirtle from Lunenburg is on the right. Frank was "wounded out" at Vimy and survived the war.

expletives), the instruction is, "Scream as you make the thrust, one, two; twist so it kills and doesn't catch on the ribs, one, two; yank it out, one, two; on to the next, one, two; and the next!"

One imagines this would be a skill difficult to manage even in simulation drills. A trained soldier may well feel hesitant in the face of this challenge. He cannot help thinking, What if? Numerous instances are on record of men bayoneting an already dead enemy in order to discover what "What if?" feels like.

9

Leave, Glorious Leave

You might forget the gas and shells, parlez-voo
You might forget the gas and shells, parlez-voo
You might forget the groans and yells
But you'll never forget the mademoiselles
Hinky, dinky, parlez-voo.

– One of the least crude versions of
the popular BEF "anthem"
"Mademoiselle from Armentiéres"

As of March 1917, Canadian troops were permitted to take their leaves on the Riviera or in Paris, rather than in Britain. For the soldiers, this arrangement had several distinct advantages. For one thing, there was no discrimination between ranks in Paris or Brussels, whereas in Britain there were hotels and cafés for officers only. More importantly, the soldier's money went much further in France. Clerks in Paris hotels were astonished that ordinary Canadian soldiers could afford rooms with baths, but it was well known that good food and wine were quite inexpensive in Paris. One franc bought a bottle of wine. Unlike British soldiers, Titus could not, of course, return home on leave. His was an easy choice.

Titus's battered Canadian Pay Book for Use on Active Service records that on August 29, 1917, Sergeant Mossman was granted a ten-day leave. This, his very first furlough, served as a much needed break before the next looming engagement – the Battle of Passchendaele. At the time, his pay book shows his daily pay was $1.35, and if in the field, an extra 15 cents made for a total daily rate of $1.50; roughly $45 per month. In earnings, the Canadians far exceeded the Brits, who received a shilling (a "bob") per day to the Canadians' five and whose term for the colonials was "fucking five bobbers." But even the Brits were better off than French conscripts, whose pay totalled twenty-five centimes per day.

Apparently, Titus thoroughly enjoyed himself in Paris. Unfortunately, and somewhat ironically, he would not come through his leave physically unscathed. According to Fischer and Dubois in *Sexual Life During the Great War*, "getting off" was a simple matter for people in this great metropolis. "A look was sufficient to break the ice and make two perfect strangers into lovers. To a considerable extent the position was the same, for instance, in London, but in Paris, which was close to the front, this sexual frenzy was more intense and widespread."

The temptations of a large civilian population proved too much for the lonely soldier brought up in the chastity and poverty of rural Nova Scotia. Robert Graves in *Goodbye To All That* notes, "There were no restraints in France; these boys had money to spend and knew that they stood a good chance of being killed within a few weeks anyhow. They did not want to die virgins."

Returning from leave on September 7, 1917, it became painfully evident, at least to Titus, that he had contracted venereal disease (VD). Despite a strict Puritanical upbringing, he admitted late in his life (to my sister Carolyn) that he "only ever had 'the clap' twice while overseas." His official military record confirms this confession for one instance, that having been several days following his Paris leave. No record of a second case exists in his medical file. Perhaps the trauma of what would prove a lengthy convalescence in hospital caused Titus to consider he'd had a double dose. In any case, history suggests that he may have overdone things in Paris.

His pressing personal problem, a minor affair in the greater scheme of things to be sure but a problem nonetheless, was diagnosed on September 15 by members of the Field Ambulance near an advanced dressing station. That came about following one of many regular, sometimes random but always deeply humiliating, "dangle parades." He was kept for a few days, but finding no quick fix he was forwarded, on September 19, to the Casualty Clearing Station, a tented community well behind the lines. It was located near Vimy, beside the Zouave Valley on Hospital Ridge – a bad omen so far as Titus's immediate future was concerned.

There are reports that the rate of VD infection among Canadian troops was one in nine, a figure nearly six times that of British soldiers. Each of these casualties was docked their field allowance and ineligible for leave for a full year. According to the 85th Battalion's medical officer, Andrew MacPhail, there were 66,083 cases of venereal disease – primarily syphilis or gonnorhea – in the Canadian army during the war. This works out to more than 10 percent of the total Canadian troop commitment in the Great War.

There is little discussion in the literature about the role of prostitution on the Western Front, although the practice was rampant. There is a long history of legalized brothels in France. These *maisons tolérées*, commonly several to a town, were scattered throughout northern France. During the Battle of the Somme they proliferated. This was an era when the French, at least, considered regular sex essential to a man's physical health. It was quite acceptable that married men be entertained by prostitutes while away from their wives; indeed their need was considered to exceed that of younger, unmarried soldiers.

Be that as it may, the French took things a good deal further and employed mobile brothels known as *mobile de champagne* to service French soldiers. These operated from large trucks containing up to ten women. Thus, even those unfortunates at the front line, unable to take much time off from shooting and being shot at, could be accommodated. While patriarchal processes and principles might have prohibited women from enlisting for combat, no such things inhibited other front-line roles.

The women of *maisons tolérées* were subject to strict discipline by a Madame and underwent twice weekly medical examinations by a doctor. Limited by the science of the time, medical examiners employed only a spatula and rubber gloves; although useless for detecting gonorrhea, this rude procedure could confirm syphilitic infection. Outside such professional establishments of course, large numbers of camp followers and amateur prostitutes plied their trade in streets and bars.

For the first years of the Great War, the BEF dealt with sex and the soldiers' way of life according to Victorian Age ideas. Contracting venereal disease was considered a crime, and punishment took several forms, including loss of pay and privileges. In some instances an unfortunate individual might be paraded as a pariah. Troops were subjected to purity campaigns launched by chaplains and lectures by medical officers on the evils of "loose women" and sexual intercourse. In short, moral and religious considerations prevented more practical solutions. Meanwhile, on the Western Front men were busily slaughtering each other on a daily basis. This did not seem to factor into the morality equation.

However, as the war progressed so did some common sense thinking. By 1918 regulations had changed, and the ability of doctors to address the VD problem became less hobbled by non-medical considerations. By that time, the Canadian Corps was even providing condoms (if requested) to men going on leave. Nonetheless, overall the arrangements were far inferior to other armies, especially those of the French and Germans.

For whatever reasons, the hospital admission rate for VD per 1,000 troops increased each year as the war went on. According to Ian Whitehead, in *Doctors in the Great War*, by 1917 the rate "was between 101 and 198 per 100,000 per month." But British Army policy gradually came to accept local customs where troops were stationed. BEF authorities opposed closing *maisons tolérées* to British troops for fear of offending the French. So, whenever the BEF took over a section in the French military zone, the brothels were retained; these establishments, in turn, accepted the class divisions of the British military. In British-controlled sectors on the Western Front, *maisons tolérées* showed either a blue lamp reserved for officers or red lamps for other ranks. Typically, the lamps were lit about five minutes before the six p.m. opening. Then the inward rush began.

Inside the Red Lamp, Madame collected the one franc entry fee after which the soldier paid the lady of his choice any sum from one franc upward. In this, Canadians and other colonials evidently had their pick of the ladies because their daily pay of five or six shillings was about five times that of British troops. The Germans had a very similar "Hinky Dinky" system, and their rate of pay was about the same as the British.

During the latter part of the war, Titus's pay as Company Sergeant Major would rise to $1.60 per day, plus 20 cents field allowance for a daily rate of $1.80 and monthly $55.80. Except for his fifty cents a day penalty throughout his lengthy hospitalization at Étaples-sur-Mer, no restrictions of pay for misconduct are recorded in his pay book. In sum, his wages for waging war would have exceeded those of fellow fishermen toiling at home on the sea. But in truth, at this stage he probably would much rather have been fishing.

Entanglements
"Come on, Bert, it's safer in the trenches."
Cartoon from *The Bystander's Fragments from France*
(Bairnsfather 1916:7).

Treatment of VD was painful and undignified. The symptoms were well known, and medical practitioners in the BEF and CEF had no difficulty distinguishing between the two main types. For gonorrhea, a treatment station supplied ointment with mercuric chloride. Far more inconvenient was a urethral irrigation of potassium permanganate to counter infection following exposure. When these procedures failed, as they often did, the case was sent down the line to a Casualty Clearing Station and from there to a hospital.

Cases of syphilis were rather more complicated, although a lengthy treatment with Salvarsan – a powerful chemotherapeutic agent developed in 1906 for treatment of the microorganism responsible for syphilis – was reasonably successful, depending on the stage of infection. However, despite the availability of Salvarsan, the treatment with mercuric cholride generally continued to be prescribed. Syphilis remained a major problem affecting soldiers on the Western Front. According to Mark Harrison, in *The Medical War*, hospital stays were on average fifty to sixty days. Some men did not care and had little interest in being cured. They patronized brothels to contract VD and thus escape the front-line slaughter. In fact, infected prostitutes could earn more than healthy ones. The story of the carnage among the women in that employ has never been told.

While Titus was enjoying his Paris leave, the 85th's thirty-nine-day "tour" in the line in the Avion Sector near Lens ended on September 2, 1917. Relieved at last, the battalion removed to Hospital Ridge Camp. They were busy training for another extended effort to hold the Germans in check south of Lens. From time to time, they found themselves at Château de la Haie, a well-remembered refuge from their mid-February 1917 introduction to war at Vimy Ridge. All the while they occupied defensive positions, working to repair trench systems and building a new communications trench. Unfortunately, the enemy's artillerymen remembered the exact locations and range of all the old ones.

Titus must have met up briefly with some of his comrades at Hospital Ridge. He would have been thoroughly embarrassed, too, by the jibes aimed at him by fellow NCOs when they surmised the results of his leave in gay Paree. I expect the exchange would've gone something like this:

"So, where did you hole up?" they'd have laughed. "You must have had a good time of it!"

"Wasn't planned you know," he'd have replied, hoping that his painfully honest embarrassment wasn't too obvious.

The exact nature of Titus's affliction is not clear from his medical record. However, due to unspecified but serious complications, he boarded an ambulance train together with numerous other casualties and was evacuated to No. 51 General Hospital in the coastal town of Étaples-sur-Mer on September 22, 1917. Here he would remain, docked his fifty cents per day field allowance, and demoted from sergeant to lance corporal, until his discharge to duty on December 11, 1917, a total of eighty days.

He was destined to miss out on Haig's Passchendaele "Big Push." It was with deep regret that Titus had to leave the battalion. He felt like he was sneaking out on his comrades. As a soldier, dedicated to his cohort, he would never be able to forget the burden he had been unable to share with his fellow soldiers at Passchendaele.

Étaples-sur-Mer, situated about fifteen miles south of Boulogne, served as the main depot, transit camp and hospital centre of the BEF. It deserves a book-length account on its own, being the site of sickness, love, death, employment, and mutiny. Amidst the windswept dunes and pine trees of the "Opal Coast," the camp was established in February 1915, as a squalid overcrowded tent city of unhappy and underfed soldiers. Étaples ("Staples" to the English, and "Eat apples" to most BEF soldiers) was, by 1917, a vast British military training camp hosting some 100,000 men. Known as Portus to the

Romans, Étaples is well acquainted with sieges. It is where Julius Caesar gathered his troops to invade Britain in 55 BCE. It was a regular port of call for the Vikings in the ninth century, and for several French counts and kings. It was repeatedly sacked during the Hundred Years War (1337-1453), and in 1804 Napoleon amassed troops here, awaiting a window of opportunity to invade Britain.

Étaples was visited by plagues as well as sieges. A major outbreak of the Black Death took place in 1596. During the winter of 1915-1916, a strange respiratory infection occurred at the army base. Researchers in virology postulate this camp as the incubation centre for the deadly Spanish Flu pandemic that erupted during the summer of 1918.

Close to England's south coast, Étaples was an ideal base camp for the Allies. While protected from German submarines and mines, it was well connected to existing railway lines. It was so convenient that, in the utmost secrecy, the BEF General Headquarters was established in 1916 at Caserne Duval (Duval Barracks) several miles to its southeast. At nearby Montreuil, General Haig requisitioned a large house, Château Beaurepaire, where he entertained French President Raymond Poincare (in fluent French), his friend King George V, and many other foreign dignitaries.

Soldiers and huge amounts of munitions, weapons and food passed by rail and road through Étaples to the battle zones. Curiously, the Germans did not pay close attention to Étaples and the Opal Coast, aside from sporadic bombing forays by airship (Zeppelin) and aircraft. Only in 1918 did they commence frequent attacks on BEF military buildups in the area, most of which were undertaken at night. Due to the location of several hospitals directly beside the main railway station, the outrages of war were inevitably amplified. Today the BEF hospitals no longer exist; they were dismantled in 1919 and their materials sold or burned. The only visible remnant of the military camp is the street pattern in Étaples.

The BEF base camp covered an enormous area and created serious problems in the daily life of the town of Étaples-sur-Mer. Troop movements by the thousands, every day of the week, while boosting local trade, also contributed to illicit dealings of all sorts encouraged by the shortage situation and a state of warfare.

Training at Étaples had a reputation bordering on notorious, earned through strict application of British class distinction and the unrelenting bullying of a rigidly disciplined military. Known as canaries because of their yellow arm bands, the instructors were non-combatant military police selected for their callous approach to teaching. The soldiers were subjected to long hours of intensive training routines on maneuvers tracks known as the Bull Ring. As Allison and Fairly document in *The Monocled Mutineer*, exercises for the troops, as favoured by the canaries, included bayonet drill in full kit, marching at the double across sand, and intense training in gas warfare. The men endured daily humiliations at the hands of their instructors and a growing hatred of their officers developed.

In late 1917 a rising tide of mutiny against repressive conditions was well underway in the BEF, and would continue through to 1919. In the French Army, 1917 was the year of open mutiny; the British Army only narrowly avoided the same scale of disaffection. During the BEF mutiny in Étaples in mid-September, over a thousand men broke out of camp and rampaged through the town, beating up any redcaps (military police) and canaries they could lay hands on. There would be fatal recriminations for many of the ringleaders who were arrested after the situation was brought under control. The exact count, however, will not be made known until 2017, thanks to a military defense ruling which forbids release of information until one hundred years after such executions.

Military authorities made every effort to keep word of the Étaples mutiny from becoming common knowledge. As it was, the war was not going well for the Allies. Worst of all, from the army's point of view, the disturbances held up train shipments of fresh troops to Haig's Passchendaele Push. At his château residence in nearby Montreuil, General Haig was deeply concerned; in fact, he was outraged. His schedule called for the Passchendaele offensive to start on September 20.

Elsewhere, mutinies were occurring among the labour companies and battalions. Just days before the first mutiny at Étaples, No. 64 Labour Company at Boulogne went on strike. Authorities responded on September 11 by killing four men, wounding fifteen, and sentencing others to harsh prison terms. Other labour companies were similarly beaten down. In most instances the mutineers were men of colour, so-called "natives," since Britain, desperate to obtain manpower, had recruited foreign labourers early in 1917 on fixed term contracts. Their Chinese force was the largest, totalling nearly 100,000 by the end of 1918. Under military discipline, all labour company strike-action constituted mutiny, and minority skin colour resulted in harsh treatment.

Canada too withheld rights and privileges to black citizens, authorizing only in mid-1916 (with British War Office approval) the formation of a segregated non-combat unit. One of the best kept secrets of our part in the war, very few members of the No. 2 Black Construction Company[1] were ever allowed a fighting role, instead kept behind the lines, preparing timber for use by the Allies and repairing roads. It was the sole black battalion in Canadian history. All nineteen of the unit's officers were white, except for Captain William A. White, their honorary chaplain.

---

1 Calvin W. Ruck, *The Black Battalion (1916-1920) Canada's best kept military secret.*

Hospital life at Étaples was not much different than military training, and was said to be more of a punitive nature than healing and therapeutic. Rumour had it that, after a week or two, the wounded were more than happy to return to the Front. Row upon row of beds stretching into the distance greeted Titus upon his arrival at General Hospital Number 51, a single-storey warehouse-style construction. As one of the walking wounded, he was quickly put to work as a hospital orderly together with other similarly afflicted Canadian casualty cases. All of their work was carried out under strict supervision. It was sobering stuff, which might normally sap the spirit. But these orderlies were hardened veterans, used to the wastage of war though acquainted with grief.

Passing through Étaples on his way to the Front at year's end 1917, Wilfred Owen wrote his mother of "the very strange look on all faces in that camp; an incomprehensible look, which a man will never see in England; nor can it be seen in any battle. But only in Étaples. It was not despair, or terror, it was more terrible than terror, for it was a blindfold look, and without expression, like a dead rabbit's. It will never be painted, and no actor will ever seize it."

Understandably, Étaples did not figure in Titus's wartime stories as told to his family. We did not know he had been hospitalized during the war. This part of his story was revealed through my recent close review of his detailed army record. In his Canadian Pay Book for Use on Active Service, the record of his eighty days hospitalization has lines drawn through it and is barely decipherable.

Titus was one among many men admitted to General Hospital No. 51; dedicated to the treatment of VD cases, it opened on June 21, 1917. At the time of his arrival on September 23, 1917, Étaples was the largest of several huge BEF medical centres. There were sixteen 1,000-bed hospitals treating tens of thousands of soldiers each month. Most hospital staff were women; some were volunteers from various institutions, but most were hired by the BEF. The total number of women is estimated to have been about 2,500. Like the soldiers they cared for, these women were organized by social class into different work types and accommodations.

Women from the working class in the Women's Army Auxiliary Corps (the WAACs) did contract work under the authority of administration clerks, their aristocratic superiors. Since the social practices of the time did not encourage fraternization, they spent nights in dormitory accommodation. They worked in kitchens and bakeries, drove and repaired ambulances, helped clean up after bombings, and maintained the graves of soldiers. Soldiers with grievous wounds remained in Étaples, their mortal remains marked within the largest (by numbers) Commonwealth War Graves cemetery in France.

Allison and Fairly describe it as "... the cruelest of cemeteries. Here lie the men who died lingeringly of gas and gangrene, without limbs or sight – the pitiful roll call of those who lived long enough to endure the stretcher journey through darkness and mud and shell fire to the clearing stations, who survived the rattling cattle wagons with bunks stacked three or four high, who faced the surgeon and the operating table, but who could not hold on to life long enough to see England again. They were buried by the professional mourners from the military hospital, ten, fifteen, twenty a day, far from the battlefields on which they had made their sacrifice."

On their half day off each week, the WACCs, or "Brownies," would go to the nearby holiday resort of Le Touquet Paris-Plage. Their khaki-coloured uniforms also led to them being called "Khaki girls." The latter rhymes nicely with *chats qui gueulent*, which soldiers in the BEF, appreciative of French, promptly translated to "howling cats."

Unlike most British nurses, who came into nursing as untrained volunteers, Canadian nurses were professionally trained and were appointed at the rank of lieutenant. Women perceived to be of higher class benefited from the more comfortable accommodations in hotels in Étaples, and, in the case of Canadian officers, in houses in Le Touquet Paris-Plage. Although propaganda pictures show smiling, well-dressed young women playing games and attending balls and concerts inside the camp, the work of nurses was exhausting and quite depressing. "An absolutely delightful site!" is the officially reported impression of the first British nurses who arrived in Étaples on April 24, 1915. In practice, a different reality prevailed. During a visit to BEF Headquarters near Étaples-sur-Mer later in the war, Lady Baden-Powell held her nose and described it as "a dirty loathsome, smelly little town." Could be she found herself downwind from the camp's incinerator, which routinely burned the flesh and bones of amputated limbs from all of the camp hospitals.

Titus's military record provides scant information on his lengthy hospital confinement at Étaples. However, the following exchange between Titus and a fellow convalescent, although historical fiction, provides a taste of those troubled times. Corky, a comrade from the 85th, was recovering from wounds received at Eleu dit Leauvette when they met outside a café during a day-pass in late September, 1917.

"What the hell are you doing here, Titus? Last I saw you, was at Avion," exclaims Corky.

"I went on leave after that. That's when my problem started."

"So, where did you go – no, let me guess, Paree?"

"Yeh, I was pissin' razor blades 'til a week or so ago. They say it's a complicated case – just my luck – lost some stripes, so I'm back to one, same as you."

"Oh ho. No bon. Well, you probably heard; Haig's up to his old tricks again," says Corky. "Word is the boys have been practising for another of his big fuck-ups – God help us – probably up near Wipers. I'm rejoining the regiment this weekend; the leg healed up pretty good."

"Lucky you – we figured you had a Blighty for sure." [An injury that would send him back to England.]

"Probably won't see you again before I leave. They're keeping pretty close tabs on everyone now since the mutiny."

"I see that," replies Titus. "Couple o' hundred arrested. Some shot. They say reinforcements came in an' managed to put a stopper on it."

"That's right. They had cavalry support, from the 15th Hussars, an', if you can believe it, a machine-gun squadron. That would make a pretty picture, wouldn't it, supposing they'd o' let loose."

"Didn't know about that, by God," says Titus indignantly. "Make a good story for Fritz, if it ever got out."

"Never mind Fritz, what about our own people?" Corky says. "Hey look, Titus, I gotta go. Might get to town again before I ship out, if I can manage to shake off the redcaps. Better yet, you'll catch up wit' us. Anyways, enjoy the rest of your holiday in Eat Apples. You don't look all that bad in that outfit, red tie an' all! See yah."

"I could do wit'out it," Titus growls, as he gives his tie a yank. It is the last time he will ever see Corky.

About three weeks after Titus's evacuation to Étaples in September, on October 12, 1917, the battalion received an order to move, via motorized transport, from the Vimy Salient to Staple (not to be confused with Étaples on the coast), a small town in French Flanders, about ten miles inland from the English Channel and due east of St. Omer. Well, at least they would not have to march. The *War Diary* reports the troops spent ten days of vigorous training at Staple focusing on "fortification of tactical localities, shell holes and craters," and practising various schemes for their attack on Passchendaele Ridge. Why no mention of trenches? On October 28 they would find out; a titanic struggle was underway twenty-five miles east-northeast.

Shortly after Titus and Corky parted company, the 85th Battalion moved by bus from Staple to Brandhoek on the main Ypres-Poperinge road into temporary billets. The next several days were spent reviewing the attack scheme. Then, in mid-October 1917, amidst heavy rain, they moved up and into the line at Passchendaele. And so it was that Titus was left behind at Étaples-sur-Mer, in Hospital Blues – a blue uniform and red tie – the dress distinguishing those soldiers of the BEF undergoing specialized treatment. He would serve out his bitter sentence until early December.

10

Passchendaele

It's a long way to Tipperary,
It's a long way to go.
It's a long way to Tipperary,
To the sweetest girl I know!
Good-bye, Picadilly,
Farewell, Leicester Square!
It's a long long way to Tipperary,
But my heart's right there.
...
That's the wrong way to tickle Mary,
That's the wrong way to kiss.
Don't you know that over here, lad
They like it best like this.
Hooray pour les Francais,
Farewell Angleterre!
We didn't know the way to tickle Mary,
But we learnt how over there.

– Chorus and an alternative to one of the most popular songs of World War I[1]

1 Entertainer/composer Jack Judge wrote "Tipperary" on a five-shilling bet to complete a new song within a day and perform it on stage the next evening. "Tipperary" was a favourite with the 85th and also popular in the Russian and German armies.

During the Third Battle of Ypres, the battles of Passchendaele were just two among many different campaigns mounted by the Allies in unsuccessful attempts to gain access to, and destroy, the German submarine bases at Zerbrugge on the coast of Belgium. Waged between June and November 1917, the Third Battle of Ypres was destined to be the last great battle of deliberate attrition of the war. The objective of destroying the submarine bases was never reached. The campaign culminated in costly efforts by the Allies to gain the ground around Passchendaele.

The first Battle of Passchendaele, a day-long disaster begun on October 12, 1917, resulted in 13,000 British casualties, including 2,735 New Zealanders. On October 18, the four divisions of the Canadian Corps arrived to relieve Anzac (Australia-New Zealand Corps) troops. Against the advice of his army commanders, on October 7, General Sir Douglas Haig ordered the Canadians to prepare to attack and capture Passchendaele Ridge. Unlike Vimy, this "ridge" was a barely perceptible rise of ground. However, the elevation it provided was enough to give the Germans a tremendous strategic advantage; all along the Western Front they owned the high ground.

At Passchendaele, advancing Canadian troops reportedly doubted the existence of the ridge until they were in a position to look back to Ypres over the sea of mud. The ground was such that trenching was out of the question. The only possible cover was in the slimy muck of bomb craters. A consolation, if it might be termed such, was that the sodden conditions reduced the otherwise devastating effect of shrapnel from exploding bombs. Officers dressed and were equipped the same as their men to make it harder for enemy snipers to pick off the leaders. The battle raged over terrain made close to impassable due to heavy rains and constant shelling.

Passchendaele's fields of horror have the distinction of being described as the worst conditions of any sector of any war, ever. Will R. Bird's description is rather more graphic, "the terrible diarrhea of war that we knew as Passchendaele." Months of artillery fire concentrated in a small area churned up the ground into a stinking morass in which corpses remained partially exposed, bloated and unburied. Soil profiles on the sides of bomb craters revealed older layers containing similar gruesome fossil remains. Muddy bloodbaths went on non-stop; conditions were appalling and the losses huge – a mindless waste of human lives. Through days and nights, wounded men, impossible to rescue, lay moaning somewhere out in No Man's Land – unimaginably disturbing sounds.

A well-known story, possibly apocryphal, tells of General Sir Launcelot Edward Kiggell, Haig's Chief of Staff, who on first approaching the battlefield burst into tears, saying, "My God, did we really send men to fight in that?" only to receive the reply, "It gets worse further up." War records tell that Kiggell, like Haig himself, never visited Passchendaele until the campaign was over.

"Further up" at Passchendaele was a destination never reached by the lumbering 25-ton British tanks, which slid off their intended path into oozy internment. Foot soldiers approached the Front along "duck boards" laid around and between filthy muck- and slime-filled craters. Supply mules and men alike drowned if they slipped off the treacherous track. Bomb craters became silted in with mud and, thus camouflaged, were death traps waiting with a grip like quicksand to catch and swallow unfortunates. This portion of the Ypres Salient was a dark chaos of destruction. In military terms this salient was an area around Ypres (Ieper), Belgium, which projected as a bulge in the line into No Man's Land surrounded in front and on both sides by German-held territory, and hence very difficult to defend.

Although carefully planned, the Allies' timing was unfortunately poor. The standard initial heavy ten-day bombardment alerted the Germans to imminent attack, resulting in only minor gains. Furthermore, the heaviest rains seen in Flanders for seventy years set in, stirring the torn-up ground into a quagmire. The situation was worsened by the destruction of the Belgian drainage system because of heavy bombardment. Worse yet, as the Battle of Passchendaele began, German reserves arrived on the scene, released from the Eastern Front due to Russia's withdrawal from the war.

Despite being banned by the 1907 Hague Convention, poison gases were widely used by both sides during the war. The French used grenades containing tear gas (ethyl bromoacetate) as early as August 1914 to try to slow the German advance, but with little effect. The Germans experimented with chlorine before January 2, 1915, although their first major attack using this killing agent occurred during the Second Battle of Ypres on April 22, 1915. Then in mid-1915 they introduced phosgene (carbonyl chloride) which, when mixed with the less heavy chlorine, proved a combination more lethal than chlorine or mustard gas. Through the work of chemist Walter Nernst, the Germans developed a gas-filled artillery shell. This proved especially useful to them on the Western Front because the prevailing westerly winds conveniently wafted the poison gas eastwards and into the Allied trenches. From that time on, no holds were barred on either side concerning the use of gas.

When the war began, Germany possessed by far the largest and most advanced chemical industry in the world. It perfected the wholesale extraction of chlorine from sea salt as a by-product of its vast dye-manufacturing industry. At Passchendaele, during the Second Battle of Ypres, in December 1915, Germany introduced mustard gas. Whereas chlorine damaged the eyes and respiratory organs, mustard gas was actually an organic vapour concocted of chlorine and sulfur (dichloroethyl sulfide) designed specifically to cause horrific burns. This widely used toxic agent was difficult to detect and remained active on the battlefield for days following delivery. Under winter conditions it stayed potent for weeks. Body heat vaporized it such that men in the trenches might awaken blind and covered in ghastly blisters.

The 85th took a tremendous pounding at Passchendaele and suffered great losses. As part of the 4th Division of the Canadian Corps, they marched to battle on October 28, 1917, replacing Anzac troops. Floundering and falling at the last, through putrid mud, from shell hole to shell hole, their ragged waves of humanity stretched thinly along a small portion of the three-mile-long front. Four days later on the night of October 31, their replacements (the 102nd Battalion) arrived in the line. A week was the most that any battalion (on average one thousand men) lasted at the front during the Passchendaele Push.

The *War Diary* reports casualties in the 85th as "12 Officers killed, 8 Officers wounded, 3 Officers wounded at duty; and 371 Other Ranks killed and wounded. The Battalion went into action with a strength of 26 Officers and 662 Other Ranks." Of the survivors, Medical Officer Hayes reported, "Nearly everybody had been more or less gassed and a large number of gas laryngitis developed."

Like its predecessor (the Somme), the Big Push at Passchendaele proved a costly exercise in the mindless attrition policy favoured by Haig. The bill for the Allies was paid in the lives of a combined British, French, Canadian and Anzac force. The tragedy resulted in more than 300,000 casualties, with roughly comparable German losses.

Haig's was an inflexible strategy which, persisting in the face of inevitable stalemate, resulted in a resonating criticism of the man. On November 6, 1917, the capture of a pile of rubble that had been Passchendaele Village gave Haig the excuse he needed to claim victory, and the offensive was called off. In retrospect it seems a cruel irony that, according to war records, a contingent of Anzac troops fought their way into

Passchendaele Village on October 12, only to withdraw due to some misunderstanding. As a postscript to Haig's "victory," five months after Passchendaele, the enemy recovered all of the lost ground.

Today, a modest granite monument to the "85th Infantry Battalion, Nova Scotia Highlanders, BEF" stands in tribute beside a cornfield on the outskirts of a village named Passendale in Belgium. Much has changed, including the name of the village that was obliterated one hundred years ago. The birds still sing, but cemeteries, vast beyond imagining, dot the countryside round about.

Before the event, General Currie estimated for BEF warlords the cost of the Canadian Corps taking Passchendaele Village at 16,000 casualties: the final count was 15,654. For every three feet of the five-mile advance, thirty-five men of the Allied forces were sacrificed. In hindsight, and with an eye to self-preservation, Titus's descendants may be forgiven for viewing his absence from Passchendaele as a fortunate coincidence.

11

"Open warfare"

But every man who had endured Passchendaele would never be the same again, was more or less a stranger to himself.

– Ghosts Have Warm Hands
Will R. Bird

After regrouping in Ypres in November, the battered battalion made its way by bus and by foot to what remained of Raimbert, a small coal mining town, for their first real break since arriving in France on February 10. There they rested, awaiting reinforcements. On the day of the Halifax Explosion, Thursday, December 6, 1917, the *War Diary* laconically records, "Dull & cool. General training. Requiem Mass for R.C. 11 a.m. at Auchel Church. The Silver band of 85th bn played at Service."

By December 16, normal strength was restored through replacement troops and the battalion was basically in recovery mode. In the process, the four companies of the battalion were further diluted of their particular homegrown family members. The effect of this on morale can be debated; some might argue that this unavoidable dilution eased the sense of loss among the old originals. Titus certainly noticed that a lot of familiar faces were missing when he soberly rejoined his unit at Raimbert as a sergeant following his discharge from hospital at Étaples on December 11, 1917.

In such times there is little room for sentimentalism and the reality of war quickly took over. From December 23 through 29, the 85th found itself once more in the Avion sector, France, this time at La Coulotte. The weather was bitterly cold. Christmas dinner consisted of bully beef and hardtack served up on the fire step of a poorly constructed front line trench listening to a veritable hailstorm of "Hun pineapples, whiz bangs, five-point-niners, and high explosives," as Joseph Hayes recounts.

Relieved at last, late on December 29, the battalion retired to the grounds of the old familiar Château de la Haie. Believed to have been the property of a German count, the château somehow escaped total destruction during the war. There it was, on New Year's Day, 1918, that the troops enjoyed a proper Christmas dinner of roast turkey with all the trimmings. Whether or not anyone but Titus realized it was his twenty-third birthday, all deemed the occasion a most enjoyable "blow-out."

Then, following an inspection and pep talk by Brigadier General J.H. MacBrien, Commanding Officer of the 12th Brigade, it was back to work on Wednesday, January 3. This involved some particularly dirty work in the Lens Sector – all to the tune of incessant bombardment by the enemy – amidst trench systems in deplorable conditions due to heavy rains. Strenuous engagements continued through April to May 6 at Arleux.

To their surprise on May 17, 1918, their kilts finally caught up with them. At last the 85th Battalion was authorized to wear the Argyle and Sutherland kilt. In early June, a year and a half following their arrival overseas, soldiers of the 85th Battalion tried them on. There must be a story out there somewhere about the delayed delivery of skirts to these particular "devils," but we know little more. No longer could the 85th be scornfully labelled "Highlanders without kilts." Many in the 85th, including Titus, found their new outfits strange at first, though they appreciated the fact they dried fairly quickly. According to the report of one Scottish regiment, kilts were not the ideal garments to be wearing when mustard gas was present.

Then, to everyone's delight, rumours of a "Divisional Rest" were realized as the battalion moved in mid-May to Lozinghem, twenty miles northwest of Arleux, for six happy weeks. This interval was devoted to special training for "platoon attacks and close order work" interspersed with competitions, field sports and entertainment. Most of these activities took place on the spacious grounds of a "genuine old French château," complete with magnificent stands of huge hardwood trees, and comfortable accommodation for all ranks.

Kilts or no kilts, army discipline hounded them still. Their commanding officer, Lt. Col. Ralston, reprimanded them around this time concerning slack performance during a platoon bayonet competition. According to their faithful *War Diary*, maintained much of the time by Ralston, "Bayonet fighting was general not good; not sufficient dash – points at bags with very little weight behind them – some discs pierced with holes not width of bayonet, showing that bayonet only touched paper … Some platoons did not charge bags."

Highlighting events at Lozinghem were the Dominion Day (Canada Day) celebrations when about 50,000 Canadian troops gathered at the village of Tinques, twelve miles west-northwest of Arras for the Corps sports day. General Currie's distinguished guests included the Duke of Connaught, Canadian Prime Minister Sir Robert Borden, and the American Commander in Chief General John J. ("Black Jack") Pershing. On July 6, the Highland Gathering featured competition in Highland games, capped by the "Retreat" sounded by no less than 284 pipers (marching eight abreast) and 164 drummers. Rigged out now as proper Highlanders, men of the 85th were a proud bunch. Lozinghem would be, as Joseph Hayes puts it, "forever remembered by those who were in it as a time when deep friendships and lasting brotherhoods were cemented." This was certainly the case for Titus, whose archives include several photographs taken there.

Mid-July saw the end of rest for all units, as the Canadian Corps dispersed to various destinations along the Front. The 85th Battalion found itself in battle at Fampoux, a few miles south-southwest of Vimy Ridge. There is only one small but highly significant item to mark Titus's activities during the lead-up to the Battle of Amiens. This concerns his capture of a wounded German soldier during a raid.

This particular incident, which he always recounted in German to me, might have occurred at Arleux, but certainly before Amiens, by which time Allied forces had the luxury, such as it was, of practising "open warfare," as opposed to fighting in trenches. Open warfare on the Western Front literally meant war conducted in the wide-open spaces. The war was changing. The soldiers could sense it. There were clear signs now that something was about to crack. This much was evident in the response of the prisoner Titus was helping off the battlefield.

"*Kanst du laufen?* (Are you able to walk?)" Titus asks the wounded man whose bubbling upper body wound betrays a lung shot, most likely to prove fatal within a few days or so, given the unsanitary conditions at the Front.

"*Nur ganz langsam,* (Only very slowly,)" is the laboured reply.

"*Wo sind ihren Kamaraden?* (Where are your comrades?)"

"*Jetzt bist du mein Kamarad, die andern sind geflohen.* (You are now my comrade, the others have fled.)"

Here, a small but important signal that perhaps the enemy's will to fight is weakening. A fresh spirit took hold of the troops as they practised platoon attacks and intercompany maneuvers in the welcoming wide-open spaces.

12

Amiens

And we'll do as brave gamecocks do, when
they're thrown into the pit at one another,
and unflinchingly, heroically
and ruthlessly fight,
till they drop and die at nightfall of their wounds,
roared on and clapped by an ecstatic crowd,
for the glory, but the ruin too,
alas,
of unpardonable masters.

– *"Coqs de combat" (Gamecocks)*
Edmond Adain[1]

The above poem sums up the spirit of the French infantrymen during the Great War. With its mix of humour, grandness, wrath and escape, it invokes a lasting image of a brave, bearded soldier (known as "Poilu") – but one who does not always obey orders. Except for the beard and the matter of obedience to superiors, the image might equally apply to soldiers in the 85th Battalion. In the Canadian Corps close

1 Translated from the French by Ian Higgins in *The Lost Voices of World War I* by Tim Cross.

attention was paid to proper dress and discipline. In Titus's case, the sense of discipline was abiding.

To illustrate, when home from a fishing trip in 1950, he travelled to Pinehurst, on the LaHave River, where his sons were attending a summer camp. My brother George, who was one of the camp organizers, recalls that, confronted by the excited mass of young mischievous boys running about having fun, Father voiced his disapproval, remarking that he couldn't see "much evidence of any discipline in the camp." Just possibly he was recalling events during the highly ordered Divisional Rest enjoyed by the Canadian Corps back in the high summer of 1918 at Tinques, France.

Barely one week after that Divisional Rest, General Currie set in motion plans to move the Canadians south towards Amiens. Relieved on July 31, 1918, following the Battle of Fampoux, the 85th set out for a designated concentration area less than ten miles east-southeast of Amiens.

"Amiens." It sounds like a prayer, a resolve to somehow prevent the capture of this strategic centre by the enemy. Arguably, many prayers for success at Amiens were answered by Prime Minister Lloyd George, who had succeeded on March 26, 1918, in engineering Haig's replacement by Marshall Foch as Supreme Commander-in-Chief of Allied Armies. Around that time too, thanks to a promotion by the Prime Minister, Churchill made a comeback as Minister of Munitions.

Capital of the Somme Department in Picardy and located on a direct line to Paris, Amiens stood at a crucially important distribution point for Allied supplies. Earlier efforts by the Germans failed to take it, but there could be no doubt about their determination to succeed this time. By early April 1918, an enormous siege gun bombarded Paris from a distance of seventy-five miles. This so-called Paris gun, *Paris-Geschütz*, a.k.a. *Wilhelm-Geschütz* in honour of the Kaiser, weighed 256 tons and could throw 210-pound shells up to 81 miles; it is often confused with Big Bertha, the term applied to various enormous German howitzers.

In the lead-up to the Battle of Amiens, General Currie devised numerous clever ruses to deceive the Germans into believing the Canadians were heading to Belgium and would not be present to confront their spring offensive. Currie ordered certain units to begin a march toward Belgium, and not to try too hard to hide their whereabouts. All troop movements toward Amiens, however, took place under cover of darkness. During daylight hours, they halted and every effort was made to camouflage encampments and to shelter under forest cover.

Dummy wireless traffic was initiated to fool the enemy into suspecting a renewed push in the Ypres Salient. Misleading "official" documents concerning a fresh Flanders offensive were purposely lost in places where the Germans were likely to discover them. And, to ensure that every soldier understood the need for secrecy, a special extra page entitled "KEEP YOUR MOUTH SHUT" was pasted into each man's service and pay book well before the Allied counterattack at Amiens began. All this, and a good deal more, was part of Currie's efforts to conceal from the enemy the Allies' plans for a possible breakthrough in August 1918.

By then, the 85th Battalion was well placed to strongly contribute to whatever action would be called for in countering a German offensive. Their location was near Caix, about twenty miles east-southeast of Amiens. Code-named Llandovery Castle Operations, the avowed purpose was to make the enemy pay for sinking a Canadian hospital ship of that name.

Llandovery Castle was on its way to England after delivering "cot cases" to Halifax when disaster struck a hundred miles southwest of Fastnet Rock, off the Irish coast. It was 9:30 on the dark night of June 27, 1918. Targeted despite running with full lights and a brilliantly illuminated red cross, the ship sank in ten minutes. Surprisingly, all 258 people aboard had made it into the lifeboats. Then, to everyone's horror, submarine U-86 surfaced and, evidently convinced that the ship was carrying ammunition and American flight officers, opened fire on the lifeboats. Only twenty-four people in one lifeboat survived. All but six of the ninety-four Canadians on board lost their lives, including fourteen nursing sisters. The loss of the skilled Canadian nurses was especially terrible. The tragedy was the subject of a war crimes trial after the war. According to Edward Knight's account in *The Union Castle and the War*, "two of U-86 Officers were jailed for four years by the German Supreme Court as War Criminals but both 'escaped' shortly afterwards." The commander could not be found and was never brought to trial.

A prelude to even worse predations during the Second World War, the havoc wrought by U-boats in a rapidly shrinking world hit close to home on many fronts during the Great War. Unfortunately, Canada and the Borden government followed British advice and did not build their own ships; consequently, U-boats operated virtually unopposed off the Canadian east coast. Over 4,000 miles from the Western Front, all along Canada's Atlantic coastline, numerous schooners fell victim to the undersea raiders.

For example, even as the 85th Battalion marched into the Battle of Amiens, on August 5, 1918, U-156, a long-range U-boat, attacked the *Gladys M. Hollett*, a three-masted schooner en route from Newfoundland to New York with a load of salt herring. After seizing the ship's brass bells and all of the canned food aboard, the raiders placed a bomb in the schooner's hold. However, they neglected to close the hatches, and the ship's hull withstood the blast. As she listed and went over on her beam ends, the deck load of 220 barrels of herring slid off into the sea.

Led by their captain, Abraham Cluett of Lunenburg, the fishermen took to their dories and rowed for the nearest shore twenty-five miles away. That was West Ironbound Island, a windswept outpost of civilization less than a mile from Gaff Point on the mainland and within sight of Titus's birthplace on the hill in Upper Kingsburg. Safely ashore on West Ironbound, they were welcomed by the family of lighthouse keeper Frederick Wolfe.

The *Gladys M. Hollett* did not sink, but lived to sail again postwar. As for U-156, until its disappearance without a trace north of England in September 1918, it was responsible during its two patrols for sinking forty-four ships, including a warship. In design, U-156 was identical to the German cargo-carrying submarine *Deutschland*, pictured on page 51, except that substantial armaments (two torpedo tubes and two 105-mm deck guns) had been added. One of five such converted freighters, the largest U-boats of the Great War, U-156 was launched on April 17, 1917, three days following the Battle of Vimy Ridge.

Unconfined by trenches now, in Caix the men predictably went wild in their enthusiasm for open warfare. Hundreds of tanks waddled about uncontested, for the Germans delayed in developing their own. Further along the line, squadrons of Allied cavalry galloped about, preparing for the attack. Essential in earlier wars, horses played important roles in this one too. In addition to carrying high-ranking officers, horses and mules powered much of the heavy hauling. Horsemen could cover ground more quickly than most other means of conveyance at the time; however, horses were no less immune to machine-gun fire than humans. By early 1918, even Haig must have had doubts about the cavalry. Nevertheless, it continued to play a minor role throughout the Great War. His faith was such that throughout the war he saw to it that three divisions of mounted troops (50,000 men) were held in reserve, ready at all times to take to the field.

Currie's plan of misdirection, ruses and diversions succeeded. To the Germans' astonishment, the Canadians suddenly appeared in force at Amiens. "We were told you were in Flanders; how I would like to hang our fools of Intelligence officers," said one angry officer taken prisoner.

Operating on relatively crater-free and favourably hard ground, the tanks spearheaded a strong counterattack on the Germans. With the all-important element of surprise, the Allies forced the enemy to retreat, in some cases, to points beyond the Hindenburg Line from which the Germans launched their spring offensive four years earlier. Led by Australian and Canadian troops of the British Fourth Army, the Battle of Amiens was the first of many that occurred on the Western Front during The Hundred Days Offensive (also known as Canada's Hundred Days) at the end of the Great War. The coincidental start to this offensive on August 8 (the eighth of the eighth) perhaps led to the poetic injustice of delaying the announcement of the war's end to a specific hour on November 11, 1918. But it proved the turning point, the trigger to the longed-for breakthrough.

Although some significant gains were made in open warfare during the first two days of the battle, the 85th paid a high price. The conflict was particularly desperate at Rosiéres-en-Santerre (Rosiéres), several miles east of Caix. Snipers took a heavy toll in officers. Officers carried only revolvers, which singled them out for special attention by the enemy. An obvious solution to the problem would have been to issue rifles to all officers. But this logic was not implemented. Despite high costs, advances continued to be made. Many were the unsung heroes of all ranks, whose insane acts of bravery, passing unrecorded by a superior officer, won no official kudos.

It was at Rosiéres that Titus, as Acting Company Sergeant Major (CSM), received one of 166 Military Medals (MM) awarded to members of the 85th Battalion. It seemed that the battle was about to revert to a static struggle, amidst barbed wire and overgrown trenches from old Somme battlegrounds. The Canadian Corps managed to gain about two miles, but it was against fanatical opposition. Titus recalled that although they had been promised tank support, the machines failed to show up.

"We went over anyway, late morning – too late really. We hadn't much artillery support, an' the machine-gun fire was pretty hot from a couple o' fortified villages up ahead. At the end o' the day we had no choice but to advance over mostly flat open ground. There was no place to hide. We were mighty hard pressed to hold on to what we had. It was hard goin'. Fritz had a clear field of fire, you."

In the *War Diary*, Major J.M. Millar writes:

222568 Sergeant (a/C.S.M.) MOSSMAN, Titus
Recommended for conspicuous gallantry in action.

During the L.C. [Llandovery Castle] Operations of 10th August 1918, in front of Rosiéres, when the Company Commander [Major Ivan S. Ralston] became a casualty, he showed great coolness and courage in keeping his part of the line well under control, and showed great judgment in advancing against very heavy machine gun fire, and, when the objective was reached and all the officers except one reported casualties he was of great assistance in re-organizing the Company, putting out posts and establishing a defensive flank on the left.

(Sgd) J.M. Millar Major
commanding 85th Canadian Infantry Battalion.
Nova Scotia Highlanders

As Acting CSM, and like his centurion counterpart in a Roman legion two thousand years earlier, Titus led from the front. He saw to it that his platoon was placed in the best position possible. Under constant shelling and sniper fire, he made certain that any available Lewis guns were positioned to hold off counterattack. To locate those snipers and/or machine-gun posts, scouting was absolutely vital, though it was not the easiest thing to do where no decent cover existed.

The Company Commander, Major Ivan Ralston, brother of Lt. Col. James L. Ralston, Commander of the 85th, was killed by machine-gun bullets while directing the fire of a Stokes mortar. Titus held Major Ralston in high regard, referring to him more than once in retrospect as "one of the best."

In conversations with Warrant Officer Karl Carvery at Aldershot Military Camp, I learned a good deal more about Company Sergeant Majors.

"The CSM is the guy that makes things happen," said Karl, in reference to Titus's career path. "Corporals and even lance corporals were gods in the front line during the Great War. That of the company sergeant major is a particularly well-respected high-profile position; reporting to the commanding officer, he is responsible for all matters of discipline, dress, performance, and morale. By subordinates, he is addressed as Sir.

"Make no mistake, on the Western Front, his duties were arduous. He was the guy most closely associated with the men in the trenches. He was a disciplinarian, but he had to deal with the same lousy conditions. He accepted orders and passed them on. NCOs like him were the interacting glue that kept a fighting unit together. His was a key combat role. He was among the first over the top, willing and able to take on more than his fair share of danger with the men under his command. He was a leader, and the men respected leaders. He had to function under terrible stress, and yet be always thinking of others before himself, even in desperate battle situations – never an easy task. Given that he had had only limited schooling, and, with only two or three years of experience in the army, your father must have learned well."

By 1918, medals for bravery were usually awarded in the field to soldiers within a week to ensure the men survived long enough to receive them. Their folks on the home front learned later about honours won by their loved ones. Thus, Letitia, whose husband had passed away more than a year and a half earlier, was not seriously upset by the delivery in late June 1919, well after the war ended, of a registered light grey business envelope, despite its CONFIDENTIAL stamp and impressive red wax seal.

Dated May 16, 1919, the letter to Mrs. L. Mossman announcing the award of the Military Medal to her son Titus reads:

Dear Madam

I have the honour to forward herewith Military Medal awarded by His Majesty the King to Sergt. T.M. Mossman.

In this connection, it is regretted that as yet no information has been received at this office re performed meriting this award, but you may rest assured it was some act of great gallantry and devotion to duty.

In forwarding this decoration I am to convey to you the congratulations of the Officer Commanding and Staff, Military District No. 6.

Please acknowledge receipt of the Medal.

Yours truly,

(Signed S.S. Wright)

For A.A.G., Mil. Dist. No. 6

Letitia operated the Upper Kingsburg Post Office in the front porch of the old family farmhouse, and was probably familiar with the military's practice respecting the mails. She probably also knew the Canadian Army's practice in announcing a death. When a soldier was killed, the protocol was, and remains, to send two military personnel to the front door of the soldier's parents/spouse. One is a uniformed officer with the bad news in hand; the second is a regular soldier, who drives the officer's car. Fortunately, it was never Letitia's misfortune to greet two uniformed strangers at her front door; otherwise, you would not be reading this.

13

The Dogs of War

My friend, you would not tell with such high zest
To children ardent for some desperate glory,
The old Lie: Dulce et decorum est
Pro patria mori.[1]

– *"Dulce et decorum est"*
Wilfred Owen

By mid-August 1918, the Germans were in retreat from Amiens, and the railway line through Paris to Boulogne was secure. At month's end, the 85th was ordered to join the Arras campaign and attack a portion of the formidable Hindenburg Line. Specifically, the target was a hinge-like portion known as the Droucourt-Quéant (D-Q) Line. It consisted of a complex trench system fifteen miles deep and laced with deadly barbed wire entanglement. Abundant concrete shelters, and machine-gun posts served by teams of five men, were cleverly situated to provide a killing storm of crossfire. An artillery corps familiar with every inch of the ground provided further support. Even at this late stage in the war, a German division

1 It is sweet and fitting to die for one's country.

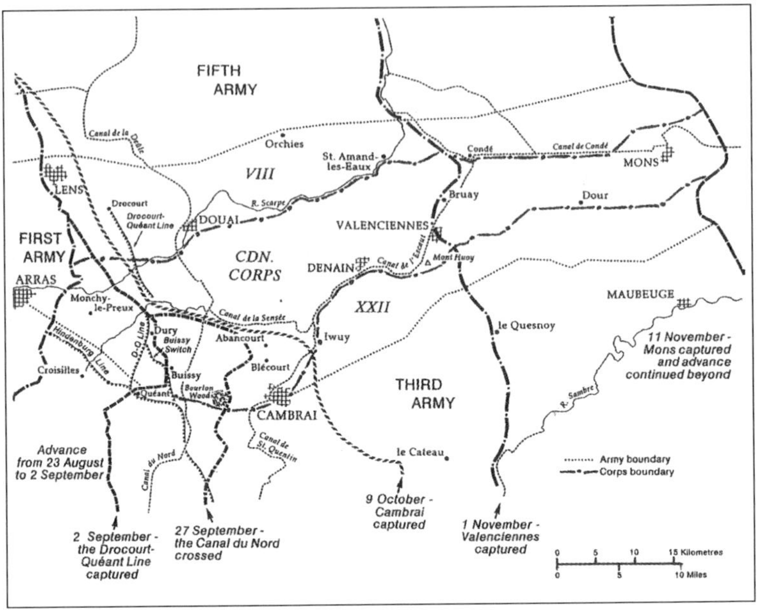

Map shows the boundary (heavy broken lines) within which the Canadian Corps engaged the enemy during the "Scarpe Operation" through to Mons in The Hundred Days Offensive; modified after Travers (1992:147).

had over five times as many heavy machine guns as a British division (a ratio of 350 to 64).

Incorporated within the D-Q Line along the Cambrai-Arras road, Mont Dury was a formidable challenge for Currie's troops, particularly those of the 4th Division, of which the 85th was a part. They were positioned front and centre for the attack. Securing Mont Dury was crucial to breaking through the D-Q Line. Nicholson notes in *Canadian Expeditionary Force 1914-1919* that Haig ignored advice from the War Cabinet about taking on the D-Q Line. He had an uncanny knack for selecting the enemy's most strongly defended positions. The looming engagement would be known to the 85th as the Scarpe Operation, although two earlier engagements which required crossing the Scarpe River bore the same label.

In later years, Titus admitted he was lucky to have survived the Scarpe Operation during the Battle of Arras. The attack went ahead as planned on Monday, September 2, 1918. However, things did not go according to schedule. In the matter of communications, especially for an army on the move, plans all too often went awry, as they did at Scarpe. In the twenty-first century one person with a cell phone can, in an instant, communicate with another, anywhere in the world. Such a situation was impossible one hundred years ago. Communicating battlefield orders in real time rarely succeeded. Radios in 1918 were too heavy and awkward for use on the front line. They were tried at Vimy but did not work satisfactorily. Although dangerous to install and easily disrupted, wires strung by either dogs or two-legged signallers through No Man's Land were preferred.

The wireless communication that was employed successfully throughout the Great War was a relic from an earlier era. It took the form of carrier pigeons, and their handlers numbered in the hundreds. Optical signalling, using lamps, flags and flares, was common practice too, but carrier pigeons had the highest success rate. Several were awarded medals – in the case of Cher Ami, a Black Check carrier pigeon, the coveted Croix de Guerre. Under heavy enemy fire and seriously injured, Cher Ami flew a key mission to halt friendly artillery fire directed toward American troops trapped by the Germans. Successfully completed, his twenty-five-mile flight resulted in saving the lives of more than two hundred soldiers. American medics worked to save his life. He returned to the United States a hero and died in 1919 as a result of his wounds. In recognition of the pigeon's courage, the French paid him one of their country's highest honours. Cher Ami, a veteran of twelve missions, now rests, safely preserved by taxidermy, in the National Museum of American History, a branch of the Smithsonian.

At the Smithsonian, Cher Ami keeps company with Sergeant Stubby, the most decorated dog of the Great War. A brindle hound of uncertain pedigree and a veteran of seventeen battles, his senses were finely tuned through experience to provide lively warnings of mustard gas attacks. But it was only after he captured a German spy single-handedly that he was awarded his three stripes. But no Croix de Guerre for Stubby, who, although serverely wounded, survived the war and returned to the U.S. to lead parades of returning soldiers. He died in 1926 around the age of ten.

Dogs played many roles: they acted as runners and sentries, and served with medics to help locate wounded soldiers. Whereas pigeons are a challenging target on the fly, dogs are more easily brought down. At one point, the Germans used dogs trained to run up to a trench and bark if it was found to be occupied; this practice was abandoned. Usually, designated canine runners were adopted as company mascots. Rather than risk having them shot, soldiers often volunteered to take their place as runners. This assignment was scarcely a trivial pursuit. Runners in the BEF were volunteers, a category of front line activity with a life expectancy of about one week.

Given these limits on communication at Scarpe, the 85th was not well positioned strategically. In fact, their designated jump-off position was beyond a 500-yard-wide swathe of ground occupied in force by the Germans. Worse, the eight tanks that had been allotted to the battalion for this operation failed to arrive on time, and only turned up later in the wrong place. A preliminary barrage being out of the question, it was back to trench warfare again, and going over in the face of intense heavy machine-gun fire.

The challenge facing the battalion at zero hour (5:00 a.m.) on September 2, 1918, can best be appreciated from the following excerpts from the *War Diary*:

In passing over the first three hundred yards of the advance, the Battalion losses amounted to approximately 50% of our total casualties throughout the whole action, both in officers and men. Among other posts holding this area, were two Strong Points and defended by 32 and 46 Bosches and a total of, at least, 18 heavy machine guns … The enemy held in great strength a general line on our Battalion frontage, about 100 yards ahead of the Red Line, as well as the Eastern portion of Dury Village, on our left flank. Enemy artillery was firing from the trees … with open sights."

The D-Q Line fell to Currie's assault early on September 2, in the face of artillery bombardment, a hail of machine-gun fire and ugly hand-to-hand fighting. It was under such conditions that Titus earned a Bar to his Military Medal, one of twelve awarded in the 85th Battalion during the war. Success in such a contest for a piece of battered earth came at great cost. The 85th lost over one-third of its force in casualties. As a measure of intensity, Nicholson notes that seven Victoria Crosses were won by Canadians that day.

Canadians were the first Allies to crack the vaunted Hindenburg Line. Marking the place and the occasion today is a modest granite monument in a small park one mile southeast of Dury. Dury is one of seven war memorial sites, in addition to Vimy Ridge, chosen by the Canadian Battlefield Monument Commission. The other six are Hill 62, St. Julien and Passchendaele in Belgium, and Le Quesnel, Courcelette, and Bourlon Wood in France.

On Mont Dury, the inscription on the memorial reads: THE CANADIAN CORPS 100,000 STRONG ATTACKED AT ARRAS ON AUGUST 26TH 1918, STORMED SUCCESSIVE GERMAN LINES AND HERE ON SEPT. 2ND BROKE AND TURNED THE MAIN GERMAN POSITION ON THE WESTERN FRONT AND REACHED THE CANAL DU NORD.

14

Nicht Schiessen!

Ultima Ratio Regis
(The final argument of Kings)

– Latin inscription inscribed on barrels of Model 1896 77-mm cannon[1]

While Titus lived, so far as I am aware, his family never uncovered the full story of his actions in earning the Bar to his Military Medal. It was as a twelve-year-old stowaway on board a schooner in Lunenburg that I learned a bit about that particular adventure. The vessel had just returned from an early spring fishing trip to the Grand Banks. I went down to the wharf to see him, for the waterfront even in those late days of the cod-fishing business remained a hub of activity. The locale was of high interest to men and a magnet to young boys – especially this one – for whom a big feed of gingerbread on board ship was always a bonus, as were any old comic books left behind in bunks by the sailors.

1 Cited in *The German Soldier in World War I*, Richard Keller.

The following dramatized retelling of a conversation I was privy to on that occasion provides some flavour of those times. That conversation was, of course, thickly accented because Titus and his friends – all local men – were most comfortable lapsing into the "deutschy" South Shore dialect. Nevertheless, when the occasion demanded, he could manage quite proper English. Picture it then: four fishermen, two of them, Henry and Titus, former soldiers of the Great War; Eli, also on the far side of middle age, had stayed at home during the war. The fourth, Freddy, is a thirty-five-year-old veteran of the Second World War. All relax in the forecastle of a vessel moored at a Lunenburg wharf. It is very late on a day in mid-April 1950.

"Any coffee left, Cook?" asks Eli, a big fellow slouched at the head of the table nearest the peak. Titus, the cook, getting up slowly, makes to roll up his sleeves only to discover they already occupy a position high on his brawny forearms. With a grunt, he leisurely makes his way back to the galley stove. No need to hurry now, his cleaning all done. The trip is over, they are in port, and their catch of "green" salted cod – the result of a two-month-long "frozen baitin'" trip to the Banks – is safely discharged ashore. Most of the crew left for home on arrival, only too happy to hand over to local day labourers the work of getting the fish out of the hold and wheeled up to the warehouses.

"For good measure," Titus mutters to himself as he throws an extra handful of ground coffee into the huge pot. Usually Titus allows coffee grounds to accumulate in the pot for about twenty-four hours. Good puritan that he is, the very same recipe is followed for tea. "Waste not, want not," Letitia taught him. Arriving from the dories after setting or hauling at the tail-end of winter on the Banks, hungry men drank the cook's brew scalding hot – likely more for heat than for the taste. In any case, contests of any sort with a ship's cook on a Grand Banks schooner were generally not the healthiest pastime for the instigator.

A schooner's cook was the equivalent of a non-commissioned officer, and in this role Titus, an inveterate disciplinarian and by nature a sort of tribal creature, was thoroughly at home. This forecastle NCO, like his regimental counterpart, was positioned to report daily in private to his captain on the state of the ship's company. This important liaison occurred when the cook, according to custom, delivered the captain's meals to the wheelhouse where that individual lived apart from the men. But in fairness, Titus was recognized as one of the better cooks on what remained, in the early 1950s, of the once proud armada of vessels in the Lunenburg fleet. And he made especially good gingerbread.

Heavy porcelain mugs are pushed forward. In one of the upper bunks a boy rests unnoticed, apparently content with his comic books and a full stomach.

"Anyone for a little somet'ing in theirs? How about you, Cook?" Freddy asks, reaching toward his bunk, eyes squinted against the smoke of a roll-your-own. He too has learned that it never hurts to humour the ship's cook a bit and grant him particular respect. From beneath the tick in the bunk beside him, Freddy produces, as if by magic, a bottle of Old Demerara. A twenty-sixer, no less, all note with undisguised approval. With a grunt, this time one of thanks, Titus takes it, unscrews the top, and sloshes a generous portion into his mug. In turn the others follow suit.

Returning to the galley with the pot, Titus sets it on the stove, adding a shovelful of coal to the fire before returning to the table. The coal dust's sudden burning crackle diminishes quickly. On the table the bottle remains, prominently masculine. The pervasive smell of tar and manila rope blends in with the antique scent of meals long since devoured.

"Ah, nothing like a hot toddy or two!" exclaims Freddy.

"Or t'ree," puts in Eli, adding, "This was about the poorest trip I ever made. Under a hundert t'ousand pounds, what's not even t'ousand quintel. Hardly can make a go of it at this rate – might be my last trip. I'm feeling pretty well used up."

"T'ank God the weather held 'til we made it in," replies Henry, lighting up. "Still for all, there was times I wasn't too sure we'd make it in as it was." Then, almost as an afterthought, "I give it another year or so an' there won't be no more salt fishin' a-tall anymore."

"Look o' here, you, you're right. You just have to look around. Soon there won't be no spars a-tall left in this ship, they'll have 'em all sawed off." Then, indicating the rum, Titus continues, "Time was when we could get as much of that as we wanted."

"You mean back during the Depression?" Henry offers, making do now with straight rum, and passing the bottle along to Titus.

"Yeh, there were some slow times for fish on the Banks 'round 'bout then. I went rumrunnin' for a while, but never made no money … bein' only the cook and all. Then we got hauled in back in about '26. Coast Guard caught us makin' a drop off o' Boston. Spent some time for that in Sin' Sin' down in the States, in Ossinin', close to New York, that was. That old jail was some fun, you. But I was only the cook, so they left me off after two, t'ree weeks. But they hung on to the wheelhouse boys a lot longer. They weren't so lucky."

"Guess that put a hole in their fish box, hey?" puts in Eli with a laugh.

"Well, I guess!" echoes Freddy.

"I crewed on the *Reo* a couple o' seasons," says Henry, looking over at Titus. "Your brudder-in-law Spinney was a lucky one. He was captain. We never got caught. She was a fine boat for runnin', wasn't nothin' on the water could come close to keepin' up wit' her. Made some good money there for a while. Spinney, he spent like crazy. Learnt enough French to get the girls in Saint Pierre. 'Voulie-voo promenar avec moi?' was all he used to say to 'em … and away they'd go! They was like bees around honey, couldn't hardly shake 'em off.

"*Reo*, she had twin diesels into her. I remember one trip out of Saint Pierre, Coast Guard gave chase off o' Bar Harbor, but couldn't catch up. We kept well ahead of 'em, runnin' full out for 'bout ten minutes or so. Slung a pile of lead at us, though. We was only 'bout t'ree-quarters of a mile ahead at one point. Bullets splashin' along 'side the transom, an' Spinney he just sits there laughin' away like hell, an' wavin' at 'em, you! Good t'ing then, we found a nice t'ick fog bank and lost 'em altogether."

"Well, you wouldn't want to go through that every day of the week," says Freddy. "Spinney was just plain lucky, that's all. Some experiences you don't get to have twice. I saw that often enough in Sicily."

"Too bad he didn't make it overseas. Guess he must o' bin too young, hey, Cook?" replies Henry, looking over at Titus. "We could o' used him over there."

"You mean the first one?" interrupts Freddy, spoiling for a good story to help make his stay on board with the older hands worthwhile.

"There's a good many I'd never want to live over, I can tell you," says Titus, ignoring Freddy. A resounding rumble of agreement about the table is followed by the inevitable question, this time from Eli, who was saved from army life by virtue of two irredeemably flat feet.

"Like what?"

"Oh, I'm t'inkin'. It was a long time ago now," says Titus.

"I was in the Sicily campaign in the last one – in signals, I was in signals," interrupts Freddy.

"The gas," says Henry, ignoring Freddy.

"The gas," echoes Titus.

"And mud."

"And mud."

"And holes in the ground for beds. An' rats runnin' around everywhere, over your face at night, keepin' you company, and …"

"And who was responsible for the whole mess in the first place?" says Freddy.

"I heard that men in the ranks didn't have much responsibility, 'cept to do as they're told," says Eli.

"That's responsibility, isn't it?" growls Titus, with a fearsome scowl.

"What outfit were you wit', Henry?" Eli asks then.

"Same as the cook. We was in the 85th Battalion, the cook and me," says Henry. "We got our start at Vimy, saw a lot of action, and ended up in Mons, in Belgium, on the last day. We joined up in the fall of 1915. Being from around here, we both ended up in the same Company."

"And somehow we survived to today," says Titus, warming to the subject, a haze of smoke by now fairly filling the forecastle. "But the t'ing I can never understand is why I never got it ... you got yours, Henry, worth a trip acrost to Blighty [England] ... once, or twice I t'ink it was, wasn't it?"

"Twice," answers Henry, indicating in turn his left shoulder and left leg. "The corners we got into! But you was some lucky. Not a scratch on you, an' that after two years at the Front. An' a feller didn't get a whole lot o' time off either."

"What was the closest call you ever had, Cook?" asks Freddy.

"You remember about the D-Q Line. Tell 'em about when we broke through the D-Q Line, Cook," urges Henry. "Cook won a bunch of medals in the war."

"The closest? Well, it's kind o' hard to say, because there were more than a few times I could o' bought it." Titus, hesitating, takes his time lighting up a Player's tailor-made. "Scarpe was a tough go. We lost a lot o' good men, an' I really figgered my time had come. We was up against the Hindenburg Line, an' t'ings got pretty bad. Anyways, we had a rough time o' it. Worst t'ing was we had used up all our Stokes mortars early on, and that allowed Fritz to work his guns more freely." Titus pauses, collecting his thoughts.

"Machine guns?" asks Freddy after an awkward pause.

"Yes, there was bunch of Fritzies workin' a couple o' machine guns from a dugout in a sap. That's to say, a for'ard-runnin' trench, on the south side of Dury. An' they was doin' some awful dirty work. They had to be taken out, somehow. So me an' another feller volunteered, sort o' quick an' not really t'inkin'. Didn't know no better, you, young, an' more than half crazy, I guess. Stupid really, more like. Talk about the t'ings we did!

"Anyways, I took some Mills bombs ... an' a feller we called Charlie, from up in the Valley – him an' me, we set out, while what was left of the platoon kept up the pressure. We figgered, if we could get close enough to the nest, we might get the job done. Well, before I knew it I was all alone. Charlie was down an' – but I had somehow made it right up to the dugout. No Mills bombs left, so wit'out hardly t'inkin', you, to hell wit' it, I charged right in there wit' 'em, jumped inside. Only had my rifle. They was busy fittin' fresh belts of ammo on their guns. So I shout at 'em: '*Händen auf!* Up with your hands!' an' at the same time I'm wavin' behind me for others to come in an' back me up ... even though nobody was behind me a-tall! Anyways, it fooled 'em.

"'*Nicht schiessen! Nicht schiessen!* Don't shoot! Don't shoot!' they hollered, throwin' their hands in the air. I didn't waste no time gettin' 'em outside an' back to our line. It was only while marchin' 'em back that I saw that I'd been carryin' an empty rifle." Titus shakes his head slowly in disbelief, the experience still fresh in his mind after more than thirty years. "Not a shell left in the t'ing! The clip was right empty ... an' there was none up the spout either! I felt pretty small there for a while marchin' back, I can tell you. Good t'ing their backs was turned, you. Talk about luck!"

"How many of them were there?" asks Freddy.

"Five or six ... I t'ink it was," Titus slowly replies, lost for the moment in a distant memory of a forgotten war.

15

Gunfire Breakfast

I am afeard there are few die well that die in battle, for how can they charitably dispose of anything, when blood is their argument?

– Soldier Michael Williams
to the King in
Henry V, Act IV, Scene I
William Shakespeare

The truth will out. And the fact of the matter is that Titus held back some details while telling that story. Proof lies in the *War Diary*. Included with tersely worded accounts of battle engagements and casualties are appendices which detail the recommendations for medals and awards. Titus's award of the Bar to his Military Medal reads:

12th Canadian Infantry Brigade

2225678 Sergeant MOSSMAN, Titus Mossman [Milton], M.M. 85th Canadian Infantry Battalion

RECOMMENDED For conspicuous gallantry and bravery in the face of the enemy. During the recent Operations of September 2nd 1918, on the right of DURY, a group of Huns made a stand at the entrance of a dugout and were firing on our line. Sergeant MOSSMAN rushed forward, killed two and sent the remainder of the group back to our lines as prisoners. This act enabled our line to pass this point without further casualties. On reaching the objective he rendered his Company Commander most valuable service, in reorganizing the Company.

(Sgd) J.L. Ralston Lieut. Colonel.
Commanding 85th Canadian Infantry Battalion
Nova Scotia Highlanders

It seems fair to include here the military's letter postmarked Halifax, June 19, 1919, forwarded to Letitia advising of her son's award of Bar to Military Medal:

Dear Madam

I have the honour to forward herewith Bar to Military Medal, awarded by His Majesty the King to Sergt. T.M. Mossman.

In forwarding this Medal I am to convey to you the congratulations of the Officer Commanding and Staff, Military District No. 6.

Please acknowledge receipt of the Medal.

Yours truly,
S.S Wright Captain
for A.A.G., Mil. Dist. No. 6

Most likely the troops enjoyed a "gunfire breakfast" of rum and coffee before going over at Dury. Soldiers in Allied ranks (with possible exceptions where the commanding officer was a teetotaller) were entitled each day to half a gill (about a quarter pint) of rum, and occasionally more when the call came. Sergeant Mossman would on many occasions have been in charge of the one-gallon jugs of SRD (Service Reserve Depot – or, as termed by men in the trenches, "seldom reaches destination") rum, seeing to it that each man received his fair ration in the ritual of morning "rum-ups" as encouraged by the military.

But old devil rum in such a setting was a mixed blessing. While it emboldened or otherwise deadened the feelings of men to such an extent that they could commit the insane acts commanded by orders passed on down the line, it also led to relaxed vigilance at otherwise quieter intervals. Some such intoxicated moments led in turn to many fatal peeks over the parapet. German snipers, who in civilian life had been *Jägern* (hunters) and whose rifles employed the finest German optics, exacted a terrible toll. Rum mixed with exhaustion commonly contributed to the ongoing general disaster. It was not unusual for men to fall asleep while awaiting the order to attack.

After the success of the D-Q Line, the next challenge for the Canadians was to somehow cross the Canal du Nord. Beyond that obstacle lay Cambrai, a major railway centre serving the Germans. Construction on the canal was begun in 1907, but the project remained incomplete at the outbreak of the war. On average, the canal was one hundred feet wide and fifty feet deep. It was flooded except for a half-mile-wide dry portion on the southern end of the four-mile-long battlefront for which the Canadians were responsible. About three miles east of the canal was Bourlon Village, and beyond that, to the southeast loomed the heavily fortified Bourlon Wood overlooking Cambrai.

A year earlier, on November 21, 1917, a BEF force led by General Byng, employing a large number of tanks, attempted a breakthrough to Cambrai. That effort fell short of its goal, though it did result in a "draw" recognized by both sides; apparently, the vital defensive position for the Germans was the densely wooded area of oak and beech on Bourlon Ridge. Caught in the midst of Bourlon Wood on that occasion, the BEF troops suffered severely from poison gas accumulated within shallow depressions. Subsequently on the counterattack, the Germans erased most of the Allies' advance. It seemed clear, therefore, that in order to achieve success, Bourlon Wood had to be secured.

In mid-September 1918, both Byng and Haig advised Currie against trying to cross the dry portion of the canal to Bourlon Wood. They were sure the Germans would have it well defended. However, employing camouflage and the utmost secrecy, Currie accepted the risk, and the rest is history. Zero hour was set for 5:30 a.m. on September 27, 1918. It would be a long hard day. Assembled at 3 a.m., the 85th Battalion jumped off in files "at 15 minutes after Zero" supported by a heavy barrage of artillery combined with a constant shower of indirect machine-gun fire. This lethal rain hit the enemy on and beyond the east bank of the canal. The second Battle of Cambrai was underway.

Although the scaling ladders they'd been promised failed to materialize, soldiers from B and C companies led the way, managing to climb up and over the twenty-foot-high earth and brick bank of the canal. Gaining a foothold east of the canal, they dislodged the defenders in hand-to-hand struggles. Wearing Small Box Respirators (SBRs), they were able to counter the effects of gas shells lobbed westward by artillery of the defending forces. The advance continued toward Bourlon Village.

Titus's battered and stained topographic map of the Bourlon Wood sector, dated September 1918, survives. This broken timepiece shows a lot of detail, possibly too much, but then no map is perfect. With a little effort one can readily identify the Canal du Nord and the Hindenburg Line in the west, and the straight line of the railway running east-northeast and west-southwest.

Less obvious, trenches (pale blue lines of crosses and dots) riddle the countryside and surround the high ground (defined by pale orange contour lines) which was occupied in force by the enemy in Bourlon Village, and especially Bourlon Wood. Trenches in the western half of the map area (i.e., west of the Bourlon targets) bear English names (Lion, Cemetery Support, Round, Herder, Antelope) marking ground taken by the Allies during Byng's unsuccessful attempt in November 1917. The trenches in the eastern half of the map are unnamed, though doubtless they acquired names during the successful advance of the Allies in late September and early October 1918.

As Company Sergeant Major and leader of Platoon No. 7, Titus used message forms like the one on the back of his sector map to keep Brigade HQ informed of his unit's status and position. These maps and message forms fitted into his small pack along with his tiny Bible and pay book. But getting a message to its destination was the real challenge. Where report centres were connected by wires or lines of sight, runners could be saved the risk. Unfortunately, this was not the case at Bourlon Wood, and attempts to communicate did not always succeed.

Using his map and a prismatic compass, Titus led his unit around Quarry Wood, several miles to the east-northeast to a prearranged location in Bourlon Village. Following orders, he established Company HQ here before pushing on for another mile, reaching the Red Line objective at 7:45 a.m. on September 27, 1918. It seemed that everything was going according to plan. However, a considerable number of casualties resulted from enemy shelling and machine-gun fire from large pillboxes and gun pits situated among groves of old oak trees on the dominating heights of Bourlon Wood.

Worse, friendly artillery fire caused casualties as some platoons were ahead of the barrage. This was a common situation given the state of communication under battle conditions. B Company took what shelter they could in shell holes and in dugout positions confronting Bourlon Wood. From there they held on through the afternoon. According to the *War Diary*, they were "under constant machine gun and rifle fire from the crest of the hill and several attempts by the enemy to advance down the hill were repulsed."

At Company HQ, Titus filled out a message form advising Brigade HQ of the situation, noting, among other things, the heavy machine-gun fire encountered while passing Quarry Wood, the difficulty getting enough pans of ammunition for the Lewis guns due to casualties among the carriers, and the fact that enemy machine guns were entirely beyond the range, i.e., over four hundred yards, of rifle grenades.

Smoke bombs were used during the advance on Bourlon Wood and were reportedly very effective in preventing casualties. Possibly Titus remarked upon this too. In any case, one of the many lessons learned during this battle – according to the *War Diary*'s lengthy account – was that smoke bombs in the future should be carried in asbestos bags because if struck by a bullet, the phosphorus in the bomb ignites instantly, with fatal results for the carrier.

Titus's promotion to Company Sergeant Major was confirmed on September 27, 1918. He now carried only a revolver, a questionable distinction concerning his survival in the line. After Bourlon Wood, the attack by Canadian troops continued relentlessly for the next six days until the evening of October 1, when a sister battalion (the 25th) arrived in relief. The 4th Division of the Canadian Corps forged on to take Cambrai on October 9, driving deep into territory formerly held by the enemy. What was left of the 85th Battalion withdrew to a staging area known to them as Pilgrim's Rest, northeast of Bourlon Village.

16

Valenciennes

We trenched, we trumpeted and drummed,
And from our mortars tons of iron hummed
Ath'art the ditch, the month we bombed
The Town o' Valencieën.
'Twas in the June o' Ninety-dree
(The Duke o' Yark our then Commander beën)
The German Legion, Guards, and we
Laid siege to Valencieën.
This was the first time in the war
That French and English spilled each other's gore;
– Few dreamt how far would roll the roar
Begun at Valencieën!

– From the poem "Valencieën"
as sung by Corp'l Tullidge in
The Trumpet Major by Thomas Hardy

Although openly negotiating now for an armistice, the Germans were ever dangerous in retreat. The battle along the Cambrai-Douai road and the taking of Bourlon Wood and Bourlon Village, which together formed an important portion of the Hindenburg Line, severely tested the

Canadian Corps. The German Maxim machine guns were set to fire only at full automatic, meaning 500 rounds per minute. As a measure of the insanity, the Germans used 32,000 heavy machine guns and 37,000 light machine guns during the last year of the war. By then there were possibly as many or more among the Allied forces. The Americans, who declared war on April 6, 1917, added 68,000 Browning .30 machine guns to the Allied cause, although they only became available in September 1918.

During the five-day battle (September 27 to October 1) to flush the enemy from Bourlon Village and Bourlon Wood, the 85th Battalion lost more than 60 percent of its men, primarily to machine-gun fire. Of 630 troops, including 25 officers, only 12 officers and 224 men from other ranks escaped casualty. During their pursuit of the retreating German Army across the D-Q Line and Canal du Nord, the Canadian Corps incurred the highest casualy rate of the war. This was close to the halfway mark in The Hundred Days Offensive. Commanding the 4th Canadian Division, Major General Sir David Watson bluntly describes this as the hardest fighting ever undertaken by the 85th Battalion.

The Canadian War Memorial at Bourlon Wood reads: THE CANADIAN CORPS ON THE 27TH SEPT. 1918 FORCED THE CANAL DU NORD AND CAPTURED THIS HILL. THEY TOOK CAMBRAI, DENAIN, VALENCIENNES AND MONS; THEN MARCHED TO THE RHEIN WITH THE VICTORIOUS ALLIES.

Titus was granted a two-week leave to the U.K. on October 12, 1918. There is no record concerning his activities during that break. Upon return on October 25, he rejoined his comrades in their fiercely contested struggle toward Mons, Belgium. In many cases, the fight was carried forward amidst overgrown years-old trenches, relics from earlier days of carnage.

The last major attack involving the Canadian Corps resulted in the capture of Valenciennes on November 1, 1918. Fierce fighting continued well after this date, as farms and houses were gradually cleared of enemy troops. With the daunting Hindenburg Line behind them, the end was coming into focus. And, with the enemy in wild retreat, vicious rearguard actions took place. Few prisoners were taken, for mercy was not a major consideration at this late stage in hostilities.

During the last days of the war, on the way to Mons, Allied pressure continued through a series of operations, including Quivrechain and Honnelle River, east of Valenciennes. At Honnelle River on November 6, in the last operation of the war, casualties were reported as "comparatively heavy." One officer, who had already earned the Military Cross and the Croix de Guerre, was killed along with fourteen of other ranks, and three officers and twenty-seven from other ranks wounded – hard news to receive on the home front so late in the war. The 85th, relieved by the 22nd Battalion at the line of the Honnelle River, moved to establish battalion HQ at Anzin, a mile northwest of Valenciennes.

On Thursday, November 7, the citizens of Valenciennes planned to welcome their Canadian liberators. Unfortunately, the event turned sour. This came about through a disagreement between General Currie and his superior officer General Horne, Commander of the 1st British Army, within which the Canadians were operating.

General Horne had failed disastrously on October 28 in his attempt to capture Mont Houy (a.k.a. Mont Houey), a wooded 150-foot-high hill which commanded the southern approaches several miles southwest of the city centre. Horne then assigned the job to the Canadian Corps early on Friday, November 1, 1918. The preliminary Canadian artillery bombardment, the most intense of the entire war, expended 2,149 tons of ammunition. According to General Andrew MacNaughton, who was on hand to direct the show, it was "measured in tons per yards of front," a measure vastly exceeding the amount celebrated in Corp'l Tullidge's song about an earlier siege suffered by Valenciennes during the Napoleonic Wars.

In taking Mont Houy, Canadian casualties were eighty killed and three hundred wounded, light losses by Great War standards. Enemy losses were much higher. General Horne might have been impressed at the Canadians' sweep of Mont Houy, but he demanded the welcoming address in Valenciennes be given to him, as commander. Currie objected to Horne taking centre stage on the grounds that the Canadians, not the British, had secured the city. Horne responded by completely ignoring Currie's argument, positioning Canadian troops at the tail end of the parade to mark the liberation of Valenciennes. Among senior Canadian officers, Currie alone took part in the ceremony, and then only because he received a direct order from Horne.

A rumour about the possible cessation of hostilities dismayed some commanding officers. Genius of the Artillery Corps, General MacNaughton raged upon learning that an armistice was reached with the Germans even as they were in headlong flight, yet still on foreign soil: "Bloody fools! We have them on the run. That means we shall have to do it all over again in another twenty-five years." His warning was prescient.

The Germans would argue that the army turned the country over to the politicians to arrange surrender and that the military never truly surrendered. The blame for their defeat, thus laid upon the politicians, set the stage for the spectacular rebirth of German militarism. Their recovery did not take long. According to William Manchester's masterpiece, *The Arms of Krupp*, following the signing of the Treaty of Versailles, that industrial empire swiftly started to retool. The heart and soul of the German armaments industry, Krupp began to secretly rearm the Reich in 1920, and by 1922 steps had been taken to circumvent the treaty. Panzer tanks, under development in 1925, rolled off German assembly lines in 1928.

Titus probably never heard about MacNaughton's prediction at Mont Houy, though I recall a comment related to the 1918 armistice that my father made a quarter of a century later. He and his boys were caught up early in the winter of 1944 in the wartime home front occupation of beachcombing in Lower Kingsburg. We were on the lookout for C-rations and other debris, especially tins of pemmican (ground dried meat, fruit and berries) for which we had developed a taste. It occasionally arrived on the tide in crates issued by the Americans for survival kits, washed ashore from the sinking of Allied shipping. While walking along the shore toward Gaff Point, Titus commented he would not have believed back in November 1918 that we would ever have to fight the Germans again. He couldn't get over it.

A visitor to Mont Houy today would never guess, and very few of the local citizens seem to realize, that an important battle took place there one hundred years ago. There are no marker monuments to that event. A satellite campus of the University of Valenciennes and surrounding housing complexes occupy the highest ground on Mont Houy. About a mile south-southwest of the city centre, Place du Canada is designated only by road signs beside a busy traffic circle. Leading into the city from the southwest is the prominent Avenue du General Horne. The name "General Currie" does not appear on any street in the town.

PART III

AFTERMATH

17

The Final Count

From the historian's point of view empires rise and fall, whole peoples appear and disappear, and borders fluctuate like droplets of rain running down the window pane as the centuries flicker past, but ordinary mortals do not enjoy such a godlike perspective.

– War
Gwynne Dyer

At long last hostilities ceased on the eleventh hour of the eleventh day of the eleventh month, 1918, at the ancient gate to Mons, Belgium. Like the stone wall that used to surround that fortified town, the gate was pulverized and thrown into the construction of a modern auto route. But it was close to that ancient marker where the professional British army began its hasty retreat four years earlier following their initial encounter with the Germans. Ironically, it was Canadians, a colonial ragtag collection of civilians wearing kilts and accompanied by their own bands, who would be welcomed in Mons in mid-November 1918 by the deliriously happy French and Belgian residents.

As recorded in the *War Diary*, on morning parade at 9 o'clock at battalion HQ in Anzin, France, the 85th Battalion received the following message:

> *Cdn. Corps 0645 hours. Hostilities will cease at 11.00 hours on November 11th. Troops will stand fast on the line reached at that hour which will be reported to Corps HQ. Defensive precautions will be maintained. There will be no intercourse of any description with the enemy. Further instructions follow.*

Will R. Bird tells of an old Cockney soldier, a pioneer (older soldiers who played important roles behind the line) working in an isolated area of Belgium during the last days of the war, who, upon receiving this message, saluted and inquired of the British officer, "Beg pardon, sir, but 'oo's won?" He might well have asked, and to this day the question is valid; the Great War is open to many interpretations.

On Armistice Day, however, no one paused very long for analysis. The mood was one of unbridled jubilation. Witness the crowds of celebrants in Lunenburg, Nova Scotia, among them Titus's twenty-year-old future wife Helen Viola Spindler, helping to burn the hated Kaiser in effigy. Hew Strachan in *The First World War* makes the point that, despite the level of carnage, following the armistice, "The conviction that the war was both wasteful and futile was neither general nor even dominant."

On the Western Front a rude estimate, not counting approximately six million civilian deaths, yields over sixty million men fought, eight million killed, two million dead of disease, and seven million taken prisoner or among the missing. William Manchester in *The Arms of Krupp* estimates that "In the course of an average day on the Western Front, 2,533 men were killed in action, 9,121 wounded, and 1,164 missing, which usually meant they had been blown apart and were therefore unidentifiable." Exact figures respecting fatalities and casualties on the global scale will never be known. Clerks of the day simply could not keep a count of all the casualties.

Concerning fatalities suffered by the 85th, a comparison with the figures for the Canadian national military effort in the two world wars is instructive. According to Nicholson, in *Canadian Expeditionary Force*, 619,636 Canadian men and women served with the Canadian army in the Great War. A total of 51,748 soldiers and nursing sisters died from wounds received while in action. An additional 7,796 dead of disease, injury, or accident raises the total number of casualties to 59,544. The total for all military services was 60,661, or 9.28 percent of those enlisted. Given that Canada's population at the time was about eight million, this translates to one person killed for every eleven who enlisted. During the 1939-1945 conflict, according to Pierre Berton in *Marching as to War*, the odds of being killed were only one for every twenty-six and Canadian fatal casualties totalled 41,992 or 3.86 percent of the total enlisted.

Titus's copy of the *Home-Coming Programme* gives the strength of the 85th on arrival in France as 846 men (compared with Hayes who gives 886), to which should be added the 269 men left behind at Witley Camp to recover from the mumps. Choosing the first number gives a battalion total of 1,115 men. A calculation based on the total of 611 fatalities listed under "Wastage in France" suggests that fatalities suffered by the 85th appreciably exceeded the Canadian average. Numbers don't lie, do they?

A more nearly correct answer to this question is supplied by the *War Diary*, which lists by name and rank a total of 614 men killed and died of wounds while on "Trench Tours of Operation" from February 1917 until February 10, 1919.[1] Comparing this number with the initial enrollment of 1,115 indicates a loss of just over 50 percent. Throughout the war of

1 The War Diary's total of 624 killed and died of wounds is in error by 10 because the names of fatal casualties in their Cambrai count totals 52, not 62 as stated.

course, the 85th Battalion endeavoured to maintain full fighting strength at approximately 1,000 men through replacements and reinforcements.

Whichever numbers are used, the effect is the same: the Great War laid waste to humankind and shattered the souls of many survivors to a state of no return. That century-old "wastage" arguably transmits shockwaves that resonate to this day.

18

Fair Maids of Mons

The Bn [Battalion] will give a dance to night in the Grand Hall at Mons tonight at 6 p.m. Every man in Bn is invited and he is requested to bring a Mademsell along. There will be refreshments served the band will furnish music.

– Memo dated December 3, 1918,
in CSM Mossman's Field Message Book

The local population of Mons hailed the Canadians as heroes. Their happiness at seeing an end to German occupation was unbounded. The 4th Division, including the 85th Battalion, remained billeted in Belgium, most of the time at Rixensart, a short march from the field of Waterloo, thirteen miles southeast of Brussels. Serviced by five trains daily through Brussels and with numerous open fields for sporting activities, Rixensart proved a very convenient place for the battalion to pass time until their departure. The regiment's pride, their 85th pipe and drum band and silver bands, proved a tremendous asset, although at first the Mons

A group of NCOs in the 85th Battalion seated for an official photo at war's end in Rixensart, Belgium. The most senior "old original" in the battalion, Company Sergeant Major Mossman is at the centre of the front row. Sergeants occupy the first row, sergeants and corporals the second row, and corporals and lance corporals the last two rows.

inhabitants were not quite sure what to make of the skirl of the pipes.

The fair maids of Mons and Brussels were more than happy to accept invitations to the celebrations. Unaccustomed to such freedom, they came in droves to the dances, concerts and competitions being held by the various companies. The men of the 85th quickly adjusted to their new roles.

Courses were offered to the men in anticipation of the need for new skills upon their return home. A teacher was appointed and instruction began for those who could neither read nor write. Courses in Canadian and British history, geography, and arithmetic, as well as instruction in various trades, were made available. According to Joseph Hayes, "Instead of fitting the unit's personnel to wage war effectively and efficiently, the objective of training now became entirely that of keeping the men physically fit, preventing them from becoming 'fed up' and, in some slight degree, helping them to bridge over the transition from military to civilian life ... athletics took on an increased importance."

This variety of postwar occupations is reflected in the content of Titus's one and only notebook to survive the war (Army Book 153). In the field, every NCO was required to keep a message book up to date. A recognized so-called "old original" and CSM of B Company, Titus's role continued as the go-to man for details. The cryptic, now faintly pencilled messages in that single surviving pocket-sized Field Message Book make this quite clear, succinct and free of embellishments as they are.

In the first half of the book, the pages are torn out. In the middle of the book are remnants of relayed orders, succeeded by tersely scratched notes scheduling men for inoculation, probably for typhoid, which was endemic throughout France and Belgium at the time. Then there are long lists assigning players and/or platoons to various team sports, "indorse" (indoors) baseball scores between various teams, warnings of upcoming inspections and march-pasts, presentations of decorations, and excursions to Brussels and the Field of Waterloo.

There follows a sampling of these antique memos:

25 11 18 Bn parade at 0900 hours March past by Companies and in Close Columns Lates [?] sport No 5 Platoon playes No 6 Platoon indorse Base Ball. No five wins by 9 runs no 7 plays no 8 Platoon and no 7 wins by 6 runs.

26 11 18 Bdge (Brigade) Inspection by Leit Gen. Curry Dress Lpeleton [?] order presentation of Decorations and March Past

29 11 18 men in addition to sail for England
Fisher
Barregaton
McLeod A

2 12 18 To Orderly Sgt B. Co will supply quarter guard and you will detail the smartest men Expedition March Through Mons Dress heavy marching order men will pay pituclar attention to cleaness of Equipmt and neatness of same

2 12 18 Their will be a Company smoke in the hall at six thirty to night their will be refreshments and all the Tallant in the Company is requested to come forward they will be assisted by an Orkester from the band

CSM Mossman, B Co 85 Can Inf. Bn

19

Postwar Games

Here hung the King's and Regimental Colors of the 85th Canadian Infantry Battalion (Nova Scotia Highlanders) April 3rd, 4th, 1919 while the Battalion enjoyed the whole-hearted hospitality of the Citizens of the historic City of Louvain.

– Inscription on brass tablet,
at Hotel de Ville,
Louvain (Leuven), Belgium

Given human nature, and the fresh exuberance of troops and local population alike, it seems extremely unlikely the maids of Mons would have danced all night. Soldiers whose loan of life had been so very brittle for so very long would have been quick to appreciate the finer things in life. And the maids, too, would have had cause to celebrate, and possibly some sense of obligation.

Although demobilization was decided upon by mid-November 1918, the troops continued to enjoy their role as liberators well into the following year. The *War Diary* records that the turkeys destined for Christmas dinner arrived from

B Company champion baseball team at Rixensart, Belgium, late February 1919. Titus is on the left in the front row.

Paris late on the 24th. As no dishes were available, a near unanimous vote decided on "dinner without dishes." Following Christmas celebrations, the busy routine of marches, physical training, drill, concerts, and competitions in baseball, football (soccer), and boxing resumed to the end of April 1919.

A memorial ceremony and parade was held in Rixensart on Sunday, February 9, according to Special Orders issued by Lt. Col. J.L. Ralston, in commemoration of the second anniversary of the battalion's arrival in France, and to honour the fallen: "Their memory and their splendid gallantry and unselfish devotion to duty have been one of the greatest forces in any success which the Battalion has achieved. To us they are not dead but live more truly and grandly then ever in the glorious history which they have made."

In his Field Message Book, Titus kept especially close account of the "indorse Base Ball" action. For the record, note that during the Great War the game played in the Canadian Corps was softball, which was invented in 1887 under the name "indoor baseball" or "indoor-outdoor." The YMCA provided the athletic equipment to the Canadian Corps, as gratefully acknowledged by Lt. Col. Joseph Hayes. Evidently, B Company won the brigade championship at Rixensart in late February 1919. The *War Diary* reports the team went on to win the Divisional Championship against the 54th Battalion on Saturday, March 1, 1919, and "the game was played at 13.00 hours on B Coys. Parade ground and was a good clean game all through." Much is missing here, including the names of the players.

However, there is in Titus's archives a photograph of nine soldiers including him, posed on a grassy field bordered by woods (page 168). Centring the group, a sergeant holds in his right hand a ball labelled B and in his left hand a sort of baton, initially mistaken as the drill cane of an officer. However, a magnifying glass reveals the name "Spalding." None of us ever realized that our father was once a member of a champion baseball team.

Titus received a forty-eight-hour leave to Brussels on March 11, 1919. That brings his total days of leave in three years' service to twenty-six. It's about par for the course, seeing as BEF soldiers merited ten days leave for every fifteen months' service.

Titus's "Casualty Form – Active Service" shows that he was one of those selected to travel to England on December 14, 1918, to oversee the safe transport of the King's and Regimental Colours to Belgium in time for the anniversary and memorial ceremony in Rixensart, and the liberation celebrations in the university city of Louvain.

Display of the King's Colours and Regimental Colours of the 85th Battalion. Titus is second from the left; location, probably Louvain, Belgium, April 4, 1919.

The 85th Battalion was the first British Unit to enter Louvain following liberation. Without doubt, it was one of their proudest moments during the armistice interval. Upon their arrival in Louvain, according to the *War Diary*:

The Belgian Commandant de la Place met the Commanding Officer, Lt.-Colonel Ralston, here and then went into the line, and paid a graceful compliment to the Battalion by saluting the Colours and kissing their hem, the highest token that an Officer of the Belgian Army can pay to a unit. It is worthy of note that the crowds along the street paid the greatest respect to the Colours, soldiers saluting and male civilians removing their head-dress as the Colours passed. The Colours were then marched off and deposited in the Hotel de Ville [City Hall].

The citizens of Louvain remembered the destruction wrought by the Germans from August 25 to 30, 1914, when they took revenge for an attack by a Belgian force against the invaders. On that occasion much of the city was laid to waste and burned, including the city library and its famous university. Worse, as documented in detail by H. Holger Herwig, reprisal shootings of Belgian civilians were widely carried out, regardless of gender or age. A totally different spirit gripped the city and its citizens in April 1919.

Alas, no record in Titus's inimitable scrawl is known which documents the details of those two memorable days the 85th spent in Louvain on April 3 and 4. An officially sanctioned army photograph shows him helping to display the King's and Regimental Colours at Louvain (page 170). A brass tablet in Louvain marks the place where the Colours were deposited.

As Canadian representatives/ambassadors, the 85th was taken to heart by the people of Louvain. Placards throughout the city called upon the citizens to welcome "The gallant Canadians who freed them from the Bosche rule." And they were happy to oblige. Tremendous cheering crowds of Belgians turned out for all events (including baseball and football games, parades, and concerts) during the two-day visit.

By early April 1919, plans were underway for the 85th to embark from Le Havre for Southampton. The battalion anticipated taking part in the march to the Rhine as part of the army of occupation. However, that order was changed and only the 1st and 2nd Divisions entered the Rhineland. Those contingents would be plagued by bad weather and severe supply problems during their three-week march to the Rhine.

The *War Diary* reports the men rejoiced to be heading home at last "yet leaving many friendly hearts behind." The battalion headed by train southwest to Le Havre where it arrived early on Sunday morning, April 27, and promptly "Marched to No. 2 Rest Camp where it was bathed, deloused and where necessary reclothed."

The final memo in Titus's battered Field Message Book concerns the departure time from Le Havre, May 1, 1919, for England:

B Co Duties at Le Harve
Q Sgt report at O R at 08.00 hour
" " 10.00 hour
Sick Parade at 09.00 hour
One hut ordley detailed dayely to see hut are clean

1 picket in each hut consisting of 1 L/Cpl and three men they wear waist belts and baynots, their duties are to see visitors don't make love to mens kit and to make then selves acquanted with fire orders

20

Passage Into History

Chase me Charlie, find my barley
Up the leg of me drawers
Don't believe me, come and feel me
Up the leg of me drawers

– *One of many limericks sung to*
the regimental marching tune
"Cock o' the North,"
the official air of the 85th Battalion

On Saturday, May 3, 1919, a "Great March of Triumph" took place in London. The parade of high-spirited Dominion troops formed up at Grosvenor Gate, Hyde Park, then marched past Buckingham Palace where, as Mabel Clint[1] describes, "His Majesty, with every member of the Royal family, stood on a raised pavilion outside the main gate of the Palace. Below Earl Haig, with other military leaders, and members of the Government watched the final scene of the drama." The route led on to Whitehall and Charing

1 Mabel B. Clint *Our Bit: Memories of War Service by a Canadian Nursing Sister.*

The Royal Mail Steamer *Adriatic* carried the 85th Battalion home from England to Nova Scotia, June 1919.

Cross, and then to Marble Arch accompanied all the while by the continuous cheers of enormous crowds of onlookers. Quite likely, a portion of the march took place to the 85th Battalion's official lively air "The Cock o' the North" (with the marchers mentally interjecting inappropriate verses to the tune).

Following supper in Hyde Park the detachment left Waterloo Station, arriving at Bramshott Camp near Witley, South Surrey, about midnight. The battalion would endure another month of "hurry up and wait" before boarding ship. Following the armistice, amidst riots in military camps in England, and the march to the Rhine, more than a year would pass before all the troops and construction battalions could be brought home.

About a month before sailing for home, Titus was confirmed Warrant Officer Class Two on March 27, 1919. Equivalent rank in the modern Canadian Army is Master Warrant Officer. The impressive-looking document, retroactive to September 27, 1918, is signed (in blue ink) by Sir Albert Edward Kemp and dated (in black ink) May 27, 1920. Kemp, a successful businessman and friend of Prime Minister Borden, served as Minister of Militia prior to assuming office as Minister of Overseas Military Forces at Canadian Headquarters, London, in January 1918. During the massive German offensive in the summer of 1918 (Second Battle of the Marne), he and Lt. General Currie lobbied successfully to prevent British warlords breaking up the Canadian Corps and feeding them into their units during the last phase of the war when British forces were hard put to maintain strength. As a warrant officer in the 85th Battalion, Titus drew his pay from the date of his promotion, though evidently the minister was only able to sign the warrant a year and a half later.

At last, on May 31, they took a train to Liverpool and boarded the S.S. *Adriatic*, bound for Halifax. What a tremendously exciting occasion! On board ship, the men heard a stirring address by their Commanding Officer, Lt. Col. James L. Ralston, on a memorable chapter in Canada's history.

In a few hours our Battalion as a part of Canada's Expeditionary Force will pass into History. At the same time we say Good-bye to each other as comrades in arms.

We hardly appreciate just yet, how much the breaking of these associations will mean to us; but we can quite expect that there will be times when the lonesome feeling for the old boys and the old Battalion will come even in the midst of home and friends, and then we will realize that the comradeships and the memories of those days and nights together are among the most valued experiences of our lives.

We salute our gallant dead. Their heroism and sacrifice will live for ever in the History of the achievements of the war. It is their splendid example of steadfastness which has inspired others to do seemingly impossible tasks, and the traditions of the Battalion are rich with the stories of their courage and unfaltering devotion to duty.

We remember gratefully the constant support and unfailing encouragement and confidence of the friends at home who have helped in our work perhaps more than they or we will ever know.

We thank you personally for the part you have played in the success of the Battalion and in helping to attain Victory for the cause in which we fought; but nothing which men can say, and no honours which you can receive, will compare with the pride and satisfaction in your own heart that your services have helped to bring undying honour to your native land.

Canada needs now from you just the same sort of energy and determination and courage in civilian life. We cannot live on the past. The future of our Country is marvellously promising if each of us will take up his work, whatever and wherever it is, earnestly and loyally, and with a pride in doing it well.

A last word as to the old Battalion. We are as proud as men can be of the 85th. It has worked and fought its way to recognition and distinction, no matter how difficult the task and in spite of losses which have seemed at the time irreparable. A parting "Present" to the Colours – Our service together under them will mean an enduring bond of friendship between us all as the years go by.

We give you our heartfelt best wishes for success and happiness.

Titus's signed personal copy of this treasured document is one of many, delivered on board ship, June 5, 1919, to each and every soldier, four days before their tumultuous welcome home to a Halifax that remained thoroughly devastated by the explosion of the ammunition-laden *Mont Blanc* almost a year and a half earlier.

Adriatic docked in Halifax early on Sunday morning, June 8, 1919. As a dockside reunion of soldiers with family and friends was impractical, everyone was reunited the next day at Mewburn Barracks (named for Major General S.C. Mewburn, who succeeded Sir Edward Kemp as Minister of Militia) just before noon. The sun shone throughout a gloriously busy and entertaining day. At 3:00 p.m. on June 9, a street parade got underway from nearby Elliot Barracks on Sackville Street beside Citadel Hill. Then, following a banquet held at 5:30 at the Armouries, a welcoming ceremony took place at 7:30 in the Public Gardens for the battalion and friends.

Too soon, it was finished. Under the direction of Lt. Col. Ralston, a remnant company of the battalion assembled at Grafton Park and, headed by the Royal Canadian Regiment Band, marched with the King's and Regimental Colours to deposit them at Government House on June 15, 1919. By General Order 149 the battalion was disbanded on September 15, 1920. Today, the Colours of the 85th Battalion rest in the Nova Scotia Archives in Halifax.

21

War Relics

Pack up your troubles in your old kit bag,
And smile, smile, smile,
While you've a Lucifer to light your fag,
Smile, boys, that's the style.
What's the use of worrying?
It never was worthwhile, so
Pack up your troubles in your old kit bag,
And smile, smile, smile.

– Chorus to the popular 1915 song by
George Asaf (George Henry Powell)
& Felix Powell

Troops were officially restricted to army issue in what they could bring back home with them. No souvenirs were allowed; however, as Will R. Bird tells it, clever entrepreneurs found ways and means of getting around this regulation. Hence, odds and ends of Great War paraphernalia (which my brother George and I referred to as "Daddy's war gear") contributed to the fascinating clutter in the attic of our Rose Bay family home. The items included a brown one-size-fits-all "tin" hat, complete with the strap and an impressive dent, which to our lively young minds was clearly the result of a grazing German machine-gun bullet (and it might have been, for all we knew). There was also a very small black leather German helmet, and it got used a lot by whichever of us was designated the enemy. That was almost invariably me, for the thing more or less nearly fitted my head. Anyway, it was the one with the shiny spike on top, and for me that was fine compensation.

There were a couple of gas masks in our old attic too, though here the aura of authenticity faded because their clean appearance marked them as store-bought items, or possibly war surplus material. No matter, we kids delighted in the scary look conferred upon the wearer, and the swishing sound as cool clear air reached our lungs through the wheezing filter. It was like being in another world behind that mask. And so it was. Bayonet fighting in mud, wearing gas masks or not, must have been one of the grimmest imaginable nightmares.

Up until the old house was sold in about 1976, Titus's huge standard issue clasp knife survived in his wooden tool chest out in the garage. Kids being kids, we learned where the key was kept, though we also knew the jig would be up should anything be discovered out of place or, worse, missing from the chest, upon his return from the sea. However, we never did learn the purpose of the huge marlin-like spike on this knife. Until very recently I thought the clasp knife may still be in the garage in its old place. But no, during an early reading of this manuscript, our younger son advised me it is now in Vancouver in his tool box.

There remains a nickel-plated brass whistle too, the very same model used by officers on the Western Front. That whistle saw many years of use with me and proved invaluable on more than one occasion. Senior geologists know, usually from personal experience, that it is far more effective to blow a whistle than it is to continually shout for help in the event of a minor issue or life-threatening problem in the field.

Possibly Titus used this same whistle on the firing line to send men over the top.

The single object (now lost) among Titus's war chest that was obviously foreign to standard issue was an undamaged German silver ring. Through the tarnish, the black unmistakably arrogant and aggressive-looking German eagle soared above the words *Gott mit uns*; below the eagle, the dates 1914-1916. Perhaps the owner calculated that the war would be over within two years. As for the inscribed motto, well, like many wars before and since, it can be doubted whether any deity had much to do with it, except to look on in despair at mankind's folly. While *Gott mit uns* was of some possible comfort to German troops, their opponents held fast to the very same creed. Unfortunately, *Gott* was unable to accommodate everyone's faith and certainly did not play favourites on the Western Front.

Titus's kilt – the tartan of the Argyle and Sutherlands – also lived unmolested among mothballs for thirty years and more in our attic. Then, in the early 1950s, kilt and accoutrements, together with his medals, were donated upon request to the Citadel Hill Museum in Halifax. The kilt was, of course, one of those received by men of the 85th Nova Scotia Highlanders late in May 1918, well over a year after their initial trial by fire at Vimy Ridge. I do not recall ever trying it on, though perhaps my brother did.

Judging from photos, Titus, though devoid of Highland blood, looks sharp enough to pass muster. Boots, puttees, round brimless khaki Balmoral cap, gloves, tunics, groundsheet, aprons (sporrans?) – are all named in a roughly pencilled checklist in his Field Message Book. Everything except the groundsheet may have ended up at Citadel Hill. That particular item proved very handy to his children, and by the early 1950s my brother and I had fairly worn it out on overnight camping expeditions in the woods near our home.

Another antique piece of Titus's equipment survives common use to this very day. Of all things it is his lowly kit bag (duffle bag). A singularly unremarkable affair, this old original has hung in several of our family's basements and closets now for nearly one hundred years, emerging for use from time to time. Made of heavy-duty cotton, it has a flat base with brass grommets at the open end to hold the draw-string; traditionally, it was used to carry a soldier's personal equipment. It is stencilled "85th" and bears Titus's initials in black ink. He used it, I know, during his sea-going years. Sea-men did not take much personal gear on trips to the Banks.

On a couple of warm days each summer the kit bag occupied pride of place, spread out in the sun of high summer beside his "tick" on our south-facing lawn. The tick, commonplace on schooners of the day, was a simple straw-filled mattress about two and a half feet wide by five feet long. Feather-filled mattresses did not fit the bill of fare called for during heavy weather on the Banks when exhausted dorymen slept fully clothed in their bunks.

We children found the tick downright ticklish and far too scratchy on our tender skins for much play-making. We pretty much ignored it and the kit bag. Later in life, however, I made use of the kit bag on various expeditions in Canada. Our daughter used it too on some of her camping trips. However, I did not notice the insignia until a few years ago. Now the initials of several of its bearers overlap.

On several occasions as a child I remember singing "Pack Up Your Troubles In Your Old Kit Bag" in company with Father. Having no idea of what was meant by "fag" (cigarette), my version of the third line – While you've a Lucifer to light your fag – was "While you usually like the flag." Nor were we kids really British enough to be familiar with "Lucifer," although I remembered hearing the preacher use the word a few times. Lucifer referred to a popular brand of match.

Relics of war, tangible and virtual, live on in every family. In towns across Canada, artifacts remain from the Great War, inevitably subject to moldering in various Legions, in museums, and in homes. Doubtless there are a few relics of the 85th Battalion left in the attics of Atlantic Canada today.

22

The Home Front

For it's Tommy this, an' Tommy that, an' "Chuck
him out, the brute!"
But it's "Saviour of 'is country" when the guns
begin to shoot;
An' it's Tommy this, an' Tommy that, an' anything
you please;
An' Tommy ain't a bloomin' fool – you bet that
Tommy sees!

– "Tommy"
Rudyard Kipling

Among the inescapable yet intangible aspects of war are the smouldering after-effects on surviving soldiers and by extension their families. These aspects, only recently recognized as valid, must figure into any realistic cost-benefit analysis. Going over was one thing, coming home quite another. There was a price to be paid. Titus's acclaimed status as "war hero" would be short-lived. His wartime experiences manifested themselves as recurrent terrible nightmares, impossible to suppress during the stupor of sleep. It was part of the psychological cost of learning to kill. He lived those very same dark nightmares on the Western Front in 1917-1918. My mother acknowledged his trouble with nightmares only in passing.

Titus's memories also shaped his response to every-day household events. Battlefield instincts, which served him so well in the past, burst through the veneer of everyday life from time to time. One may imagine that these events are firmly imprinted upon the memories of a subsequent generation, in a form of heritable post-traumatic stress disorder (PTSD).

Ours was a typical old kitchen toaster and, like several early models, it lacked a timing device. Predictably, the toast all too often became "toast." Each and every time, the Battle of Scarpe or Bourlon Wood would result. On a scale of decibels, his rage would not have been out of place in the heat of action at Amiens, and it never made a good start to the day.

Similarly, other common accidents such as the sudden noisy smashing of a dish, or dishes, would trigger an eruption of verbal and physical fury. At such times it seemed to me that, terrified as I was of my father's temper, Mother threw caution to the wind in her swift counterattack. Perhaps she should have known better, but for some unfathomable reason she didn't. Good Christian soldier that she was, I must suppose that she didn't quite appreciate where he had been and what he had been through. Thus, chiding Titus for his rage, she would further admonish him. It might have seemed to an outside observer that as an academic, she did not properly respect his station in life and the type of work he did. After all, it's a common enough stereotype. The result was a viciously sustained and high-volume verbal joust between the two of them.

By far the worst insult launched was when she called him "some old company sergeant major," a particularly cruel thrust. Whenever I heard this, I felt physically diminished by fear, for I knew what was coming – much more of the same, only worse. Yet further pokes and barbs – not altogether obliquely directed – might remind the former CSM of his lowly status in life. The most common of these was a derogative reference to his upbringing in the "back of beyond" – possibly true to a degree, but poorly chosen nonetheless, because her mother (Clara Augusta) was born and brought up in the woods of Upper Kingsburg on the other side of the hill from Titus. Divorce, unheard of at the time in this community, was never an option. Titus's loyalty to country was a proven thing, that to community likewise. And he remained committed to his family.

Reflecting a lack of understanding and respect for the man himself, her taunting poured more fuel on old slow-burning fires, invisible but nonetheless real – highlighting distinction between an important person during war and a tragic figure postwar, mocked in his own house and home. Thus vigorously stoked, the fire of domestic rage built quickly. Without a doubt, Helen Viola greatly imperilled herself and those around her on such occasions. Surely she knew that CSMs are not chosen from the ranks for their jollity and compassion. Even so, like shell shock, there were lasting physiological impacts. It was extremely unsettling for all involved, especially for children, walled in by such crises and unpredictability.

There were times I came close to tackling my father, and would have been glad to see him dead, or at the very least incapable of further outrage. As a child I felt deeply confused and in part responsible for those outbursts of violence. Fortunately, none of us ever completely lost control. But at times it was a very near thing.

I shiver even yet recalling some of those awful confrontations. My sister tells me that as a teenager she would get up and leave the house when domestic strife threatened to run out of control. She recalls Mother remonstrating with Titus that they had to stop fighting or the children would not want to come home for visits. I do not recall ever leaving a scene of domestic violence between my parents, though it might have been the best option. On the worst such occasions, Titus followed up the argument by vehemently uttering threats to do himself in. Some pretty realistic scenarios were proposed. One was to drown himself in our cesspool, as a septic tank was known in those days. The prospect of anyone trapped in this cistern of human waste was absolutely horrifying.

An immovable fixture common in rural communities, the cesspool unfortunately slouched near at hand, waiting as it were, in clear view from our kitchen windows. The last time I passed by the old house I saw that it's still there. It's a large concrete bunker buried close beside the south side of the driveway, protruding about a foot above ground. Much like a Great War pillbox perhaps, except for its relatively thin concrete walls and a large square opening on top, it looks to be still capped with a rough platform of unfinished and unpainted boards weighted down with a few rocks and iron bars – a crude cover easily removed.

Such was the intensity of Titus's fits and the depths of his doubts and despondencies that on one occasion in the late 1950s, when he failed to appear for our precise five o'clock suppertime, I was delegated in the dark of early evening to check the cesspool to see whether he had jumped in. He never did. But he had done most of the pick and shovel work to create the thing. He knew it was over six feet deep. And he was no swimmer.

In hindsight one can speculate whether, despairing of his future, Titus was reminded of the bloody bogs of No Man's Land which he had somehow survived, and for what? Of course, it never occurred to me as a child to think of this and of possible connections to my father's wartime experiences, particularly as that past was largely hidden.

That Titus's dysfunctional behaviour corresponds to PTSD, a psychological disorder brought on by traumatizing experiences outside the normal, comes as no surprise. Linked with domestic violence, suicide, homelessness, substance abuse, and crime, officially recognized symptoms include reliving events, avoidance (e.g., feeling you have no future), and arousal (e.g., sudden rage). Some soldiers are said to be more susceptible than others to PTSD. Prior to the Vietnam War, it went by other names. During the Great War it was called "shell shock" or, worse, cowardice. Caroline Alexander[1] explains that early in the war shell shock was "deemed to be a physical injury, and the shellshocked soldier was thus entitled to a distinguishing 'wound stripe' for his uniform, and to possible discharge and a war pension. But by 1916, military and medical authorities were convinced that many soldiers exhibiting the characteristic symptoms … had been nowhere near exploding shells."

By late 1917 the term fell out of favour with authorities, and on the advice of psychiatrists, medical opinion reclassified the afflicted as "Not Yet Diagnosed Nervous" (NYDN). Soldiers promptly redefined the acronym as "Not Yet Dead Nearly." Following a lengthy study, the British War Office Committee concluded in 1922 that shell shock did not exist but simply consisted of several known illnesses. Dr. Andrew MacPhail, head of the Canadian Army Medical Corps, held to the same opinion, reporting late in the war that "Shell shock is a manifestation of childishness and femininity."

Because PTSD at the time was a not-yet-diagnosed psychiatric disorder, numerous men who panicked or lost control during bombardments and ran from the Front were labelled deserters. According to British Military Law under which Canadians fought, these deserters were summarily blindfolded and shot at dawn. This was the fate of at least twenty-five Canadian soldiers. Men could be shot because of their stress and blind fear, or for falling asleep while on sentry duty. The final signature on those death warrants of BEF soldiers was that of Douglas Haig. Eighty-three years after the war ended, the Canadian government formally apologized on December 11, 2001. Despite the Commander-in-Chief's urgings, even

---

1 Caroline Alexander "The Shock of War," *Smithsonian* September 2010.

during the Étaples mutiny, the Australian government never allowed their troops to be executed by the BEF.

In common with other soldiers, Titus could only communicate well with men who had shared his experiences. The understanding called for is incomprehensible to those who have not seen active service. Put simply, the folks who remained in Nova Scotia during the Great War could never understand what soldiers went through in France and in Flanders. Titus may have found some refuge in the hierarchical and risky work at sea, but on the home front, and in his civilian life, he was destined to remain alone, hostage to his memories, misplaced and misunderstood much of the time for the duration.

A well-founded theory exists that each child of a marriage experiences different parents. Younger by six years from my sister and four from my brother, I speak here only for myself. At home Titus tended to be moody and uncommunicative. He seldom spoke during meals, and was certainly not given to demonstrations of love and affection, possibly regarding such as a show of weakness. Mother had no such inhibitions, and tended to be quite the opposite.

Although always ready to lend a hand to someone in need, Titus was not one to be pushed about. And he was ever ready to stand up on principle for the underdog. As a former CSM, he certainly did not lack the voice to speak up for himself, or for others. He could curse extraordinarily fluently as well – no surprise there – although fortunately at home this talent was seldom employed. In this respect he came from the same school as his commanding officer Lt. General Currie who, according to reports, "demonstrated affluent command of the scabrous side of military vocabulary." Doubtless Titus honed this ability honestly enough in the trenches where profanity of the worst kind was the norm.

When in a bad mood he warranted a wide berth. I recall one incident on the Lunenburg waterfront the morning after my night on board the schooner. Titus might have been a bit hungover, but not so much that I noticed. We had made it up to Montague Street when a seaman from some other ship hailed him and invited him to go halves on buying a bottle. Now Titus had no great aversion to rum – on the contrary. But we were headed for home, and he politely declined the invitation. The seaman, possibly somewhat more hungover than my father, responded with a careless "OK, tight ass." Not a savoury play of words on a man's first name. At this point, the old kit bag was handed to me and the ex-CSM addressed the insult with his knuckles. I think that had I not been present, the fellow might have been laid up ashore for much longer than he had planned on.

Titus always kept at least two bottles of rum at home, and well hidden. This was a throwback to his rumrunning days when it was illegal to keep non-prescription liquor at home. Some habits are hard to shake. A flask-shaped Mickey fitted very nicely into the lowermost drawer in the kitchen closet next to the stove, where it kept company with his precious set of cobbling lasts. A larger bottle occupied a hidey-hole beneath the removable fifth step leading down to our unfinished cellar. Despite this, to my recollection he was seldom in his cups.

At the foot of those cellar steps dwelt the furnace, and in various dark far corners, our winter wood and coal supply. Round about in the darkness numerous bogeymen lay in wait, as real in my child's mind as breathing. I dodged them daily in late fall and winter, because Mother appointed me stoker when her husband was away at sea and my brother and sister away at college. Could be she had hobgoblins of her own.

As a child, mine was a fearful respect of Titus. His homecoming after a trip to sea was always a cause for concern on my part. Following the preliminaries of greeting his wife and a visit to stock his cellar cache, he would set out to tour the grounds of his modest half-acre estate. A particularly careful check was made around the garage, to determine whether I had learned the lesson delivered on a previous occasion after an extensive knife-throwing session in which I used the large garage door as target. His tools were examined carefully too, for anything out of place. If he considered that disciplinary action was called for, interrogation resulted and, as often as not, retribution. At such times it was best that sons could not be located. Spanking or strapping children was the norm in those times, and although worse was threatened on some occasions, the storms usually blew over fairly quickly.

My brother George recalls one terrifying experience in our old cellar where he narrowly escaped a beating with a block of wood. Round and round the furnace went the chase, first one way, then the next ... on and on for several anxious minutes. Finally, unable to catch his son, Titus broke off the chase, his taunts following George as the child retreated upstairs to Mother. In response to his wife's subsequent upbraiding, in a surprising change of mood, Titus blurted, "Do you want me to leave?"

Within the small conservative community of Rose Bay, Titus was known as a hard worker, a disciplinarian, and thoroughly set in his ways. It was generally acknowledged that he had a "short time fuse." But he was also regarded as a solid family man of the times, being a reliable breadwinner and in some respects a community leader. Initiated into the local chapter of the IOOF (Independent Order of Odd Fellows) on November 6, 1924, he rose through the ranks of this venerable and benevolent organization to hold the top position as Noble Grand in Confidence Lodge No. 6 in 1932 and 1933.

However, for all his foibles and chequered background, Titus remained an extraordinarily private person. He was never readily persuaded to hold forth in public. A notable exception occurred during a reunion of the 85th Battalion at Annapolis Royal in 1964 when he agreed to address the gathering. The only record of that speech occurs as a brief comment in my mother's sixteen-page *Memories*: "On that occasion Titus was called upon to make a speech. He did it well and I was quite proud of him."

I am not aware of letters exchanged between my parents during Titus's years of active service. Nor is there any evidence of letters exchanged between Titus and his parents. Most likely this lack of evidence is due to the passage of time and the disruption of war, rather than an actual absence of communication. After all, the army encouraged soldiers to write home, and made every effort to ensure that letters and parcels were delivered to the Front efficiently, the better to aid morale. Letitia Mossman ran the post office in Upper Kingsburg and most likely wrote regularly to her two sons, Titus and Dennis, on the front lines of a distant war. Of that correspondence, sadly, there is no record. Her elegant Germanic script survives on a single inconsequential domestic memo, fluent, though generously sprinkled with misspellings. Of Papa Albert's writing nothing whatever survives, not even the outline of a sermon.

Titus's marriage to Helen Viola Spindler was delayed thirteen years from the time he joined up. My mother's *Memories* records they knew each other several years before he headed overseas. This was normal in such small rural neighbouring communities as Rose Bay and Kingsburg – especially given only four years age difference between them. At war's end, Helen was on hand to greet Titus upon his return home. She tells briefly of a "suitable party" held at the old homestead in Upper Kingsburg for "the boys who survived," including Titus and a close relative, Lawrence Mossman. In what would now pass as classic understatement, and blessed with a senior's hindsight, she observed, "Then it was but 1919 and the country's youth weren't advanced enough to mingle and enjoy the frivolities of life on a scale possible in later years. Were I in that old time group once again I see myself acting differently."

Unfortunately for Titus's financial situation, his medals (unlike, for example, the Distinguished Service Medal) did not merit any cash award. Discharged on June 15, 1919, as a single man without dependents, his payout was exactly $420, that being the figure for three years' service. He might also have received some additional pay as Warrant Officer, although that perk lapsed upon his discharge. The possibility remains that with his Warrant Officer Class Two certificate in hand, Titus might have been eligible to apply for a postwar position in the Canadian Forces. Given his traumatic experiences on the Western Front, odds are that he had second thoughts about a further career in the military.

For physically disabled veterans there were pensions, medical treatment, and a chance for vocational training. The policy of a one-time payment to physically unscathed returning servicemen shows a lack of foresight for the real economic dislocation which followed war's end. The Veterans Charter would appear a quarter of a century later, in 1944, by which time Ottawa policy-makers were giving the process of demobilization their close attention. The New Veterans Charter initiated on April 1, 2006, has been much criticized by a new generation of soldiers and war veterans.

Legions of women who served as nurses and as various service personnel fared little better; however, with the passage of the Military Voters Act into law on August 29, 1917, women with a link to a soldier overseas could vote federally. By late 1919, nearly all Canadian women gained the long overdue privilege of the federal vote.

Titus returned to his role as seaman for almost nine years before committing to marriage on September 20, 1928. The wedding took place in the United Church parsonage at Trinity United, Rose Bay. Ten years earlier to the day, he was maneuvering with the 85th Battalion preparatory to the assault on Bourlon Village. And Helen Viola, diploma in hand from the Province of Nova Scotia to teach Rural Science, began a teaching assignment at West Northfield, Nova Scotia.

Titus and Jack the dog relax in a hammock slung in the Spindler family orchard, Lower Rose Bay, c. 1928.

During his off and on years of courting, Titus became expert at making do with straw ticks both at sea and ashore. This facility developed through necessity when he and Helen Viola saw fit to have him sleep over from time to time in Lower Rose Bay at the Spindler home. Morals and ethics being what they were in Lunenburg County in 1919, his sleepovers were spent in the family barn. In France and Flanders this class of accommodation, no matter how run-down, was relative luxury to a soldier fresh from the trenches. Titus bedded down quite happily with other fellow creatures, none among them closer to the former soldier than Jack, the Spindler family's dog. A photo in an early family album shows Titus in a hammock slung in the Spindler orchard, wearing something very close to the old army "devil-may-care" look on his face; Jack keeps close company.

My sister Carolyn tells me that Father joked about being sent to the Spindler barn for the night. "Overseas," he'd say to his future wife, "my girlfriends used to treat me better."

Titus and Helen Viola on their honeymoon trip near Cape Blomidon in the Annapolis Valley, September 1928.

To Mother's further annoyance, he'd also make sure to mention that they called him "Tom" because they found it hard to pronounce his first name. In truth, this term was used by French and Belgian women towards troops in the BEF in general. Thanks to Kipling's poem "Tommy," English soldiers had long been referred to as "Tommies."

For their honeymoon, Titus and Helen Viola travelled in style in her brand new Pontiac to the Annapolis Valley. The car was a prize Mother had won for selling more subscriptions to the Halifax *Herald* than anyone else in Nova Scotia. Winning a car is a big deal in any age, and it was especially so back in 1928. Unhappily, a few weeks later, the young couple met with disaster during a trip to Halifax to select furniture for their newly purchased home in Upper Rose Bay. From *Memories*: "a collision between the Pontiac and an oncoming Halifax car brought our errand to a halt. Passing friends rescued and returned us to Rose Bay but it was a long time until we could function normally again." Titus had been the driver. That's the sum total of what we know about that particular incident. It was never a popular subject for discussion.

It was twenty years before my parents acquired another automobile. During that interval their driving ability improved very little. Neither of them seemed to understand the working of a gasoline engine, nor the role played by gears in the entire operation, especially the function of the clutch. Travelling with either of them at the wheel was a traumatic experience for all passengers.

In the mid-1950s, in otherwise sleepy Rose Bay, Titus again totalled the family car, a tiny English Prefect. While carelessly backing out onto the road from the post office at the Crossroads in Upper Rose Bay, he was broadsided by an oncoming vehicle. Although the Prefect was a wreck, he shook off the shock, refused assistance, and walked the half-mile south to his home, arriving just in time for the midday meal. Eating quickly, as was his habit, he said little in answer

A formal photograph, c. 1968, of Titus and Helen Mossman.

to Mother's questioning, except that he had left the car at the Crossroads. His Prefect had been struck by a large American vehicle driven by a prosperous sea captain from Upper Kingsburg. Worse, it turned out that Titus was in the wrong. Physically, there were some pretty impressive body bruises, cracked ribs, and a broken collarbone. In truth, however, the entire incident was a painful, expensive, and presumably deeply embarrassing experience.

The age of sail was long past. Now it was everything from coasters to freighters, and although the hours were still not counted, his income was steadier than during earlier times. In those days, Mother kept the score, kindly terming many of his fishing trips "not very rewarding financially." Even so, he was fortunate then, because as cook he might have received a very small daily allowance while at sea, no matter whether any fish were caught or not. Normally, of the total value of fish caught, every man received a portion. Recall that Titus left off fishing for fighting back in 1915 when, as 222568 Rifleman Mossman, he was at least guaranteed $1.10 per day; his lesser pay as a fisherman at the time may have had something to do with that decision. Late in the war, his wage soared to $1.60 per day, and as much as $1.80 if in the field, risking life and limb and everything by the minute. For all that, it was poor compensation for the weight of war experiences he couldn't talk about, and memories he could not share.

23

Flashbacks

Circumstances rule men;
Men do not rule circumstances.

– Herodotus
Histories, Book 7, Chapter 49
484 BCE-425 BCE

Born a staunch Methodist in Lower Rose Bay, Helen Viola chose a teaching career, just like her mother Clara Augusta Spindler (née Schnare). Clara's Certificate and License as a Public School Teacher reads "October 17, 1890, being the fifty-fourth year of the reign of Her Majesty Queen Victoria." After graduating from Lunenburg County Academy with grade eleven in 1913, Helen Viola completed grade twelve at Colchester Academy in Truro. This luxury far from home came at the cost of a prize ox sold by her father, John Soloman Spindler. Next, she taught in Lower Rose Bay from 1914 to 1916 before returning to Truro to attend Nova Scotia Teachers College (a.k.a. the Provincial Normal College) from which she graduated Superior First Rank, with distinction on June 21, 1917. Following assignments at various schools in

Lunenburg County, she moved in 1921 to the United States where she taught until 1925 at Oceanside, Long Island, New York. While in the U.S. she found time for extra instruction in Piano Technique and Harmony at Columbia University in 1919; then, a winter course on Educational Theory and Educational Psychology at that same school in 1924-1925. Mother's higher education was not restricted to the secular realm. While in New York, she also served as the First Vice President of the Department of Spiritual Work in the Epworth League, a youth order of the United Methodist Church.

In comparison to her betrothed, Helen Viola was very well educated indeed. In the lead-up to marriage, she did her utmost to help Titus find work in the States, but his lack of formal education, or a recognized trade, made things difficult. On this front Titus is a tragic figure. He tried out in a laundry business on Long Island operated by one of Helen's friends, but quickly decided that he was not going to spend his life as a "washer woman." No better luck was met while on a job hunt in Boston.

Then in 1924, he travelled by rail to Western Canada to assist in the grain harvest, but after several months as a farmhand near Saskatoon, Saskatchewan, he returned to his roots. Although he remained sensitive to his backwoods lack of education, Titus settled inexorably into his role as seaman and ship's cook. Like Ishmael in Melville's *Moby Dick*, it was a way of life he knew, a ceaseless and repetitive earthly effort. One trip ends, only to begin another. It seemed he recognized his place in the world despite any disillusionment. Nor was he ever heard to bemoan his lot in life.

Outside of the local Odd Fellows meetings, and regular visits to close family members, especially over Christmas and New Year's, Titus's social life centred on "loafing." This particular form of social interaction was especially important in rural communities in Lunenburg County until the advent of television in the 1950s. In Upper Rose Bay, A.B.'s (Arthur B. Lohnes's) small general store was the magnet for local loafers on Saturday evenings. Especially popular in winter, the locals, exclusively male, gathered there around the pot-bellied stove. Titus was an insider here, and totally at home, amidst the sweltering heat and cigarette smoke. It was a small store, and the rendezvous was that of intimate rustics – mostly shipmates who had been thoroughly tossed and turned about within the cloistered confines of many fuggy fo'c's'les. They were used to keeping close quarters. Young boys dropped in too, for they were a part of the general give and take, and there was little else for them to do on a Saturday evening before Foster Hewett's hockey broadcast.

Mother kept pretty good track of the days after Titus got home. He was always at his best when gainfully occupied. At times I recall being embarrassed on his behalf because after two weeks or so (except in midwinter), she would remind her husband that so-and-so (one or more of the many local sea captains) was reportedly looking for a cook for an upcoming trip. Although we had no phone until the mid-1950s, thanks to her social rounds she seemed to know exactly what was going on in the community. My implicit understanding was that she had an ulterior motive for regularly launching Titus at sea, quite apart from any anticipated monetary gain from a fishing trip.

As ship's cook Titus had very little time to himself. And he might have preferred it this way. At home, following a trip, he often spent entire mornings incommunicado in his armchair – staring out to sea, twitching from time to time as in near sleep, lost in mood shifts from which neither wife nor children were much inclined to disturb him. Puzzled, we children, perhaps unfairly, felt somewhat left out.

On one occasion my brother and I plucked up the courage to disturb him. We reckoned we were top-gun squirrel and rabbit hunters, and during fall and winter regularly supplemented our meagre allowances by selling squirrel pelts to E.I. Angus Co. for, on average, about thirty-five cents a pelt. BB guns in hand, we confronted Father.

"Want to come along with us to check our snares?" we respectfully invited the slumped figure in the slowly rocking chair.

"Eh? What?" he exclaimed, jarred suddenly out of his trance. But the spell was broken. Happy to join us along our traplines, he jumped up and dressed for the hunt, later marvelling how well we knew all the paths in the woods. Characteristically, he never hesitated in giving credit where he felt credit was due. For him, our making sense of a maze of animal paths may have seemed similar to a soldier's learning the exact layout of trenches, an ability essential for survival on the Western Front.

Throughout his later life, the nature of Titus's work fairly precluded close father-son bonding. Consequently, Captain Winfred (Spinny) Spindler ("Uncle Teddy" to us), he of the *Reo* rumrunner, was surrogate father to George and me. A lifelong shore fisherman, Uncle Teddy was a veritable magnet for us, and we followed him about relentlessly in most of our spare moments. Titus was well aware of this and, though jealous, was completely powerless to do anything about it. At the peak of the rumrunning era during the 1930s, Titus had apparently expressed an interest in going with his brother-in-law Captain Spindler. In an interview with Uncle Teddy taped years later by his daughter Faye, Captain Spindler explains that "I didn't want to take Titus rumrunning with us because he was too cranky." In any case, Titus was denied a berth on the *Reo* and was never shipmates with his brother-in-law.

At times, ours was not a particularly happy household, nor a generally welcoming one for visitors. For example, that same Captain Winfred Spindler, although especially popular with his niece and nephews, rarely dropped in to visit. I was aware of a certain breakdown here, a nameless family dysfunction. But there was no explaining it.

It did not occur to me at the time that my father might also have nursed a quiet resentment of the success and public respect accorded to local sea captains. Drawn from the same peer group as Titus, their status in the community was perhaps an embarrassing contrast with his lowly station. Used to giving orders from a position of authority during the war, Titus now ate humble pie. Quite apart from the bad luck he experienced during rumrunning, he may have been envious of the money they made. He saw how some captains got rich. Following a voyage to the Banks, for example, the men sometimes received their share of the profit from the captain's hand, dockside. That individual, having been paid directly by head office, might position himself on the wharf in plain view before he ceremoniously paid off the men, peeling the bills from a great wad pulled from his pocket. Other than that ritual, there was no paper trail of the transaction, and no comebacks.

Despite his grumpy postwar demeanour, Titus maintained a sporadic sense of good humour. A classic instance of this occurred one New Year's Eve in 1947 on the occasion of his fifty-third birthday. Such celebrations were generally low-key affairs, scarcely flagged for focus amidst the tinsel trimmings of the twelve days of Christmas. But this year, Helen Viola decided things would be different and she planned a proper surprise birthday party for her husband. Accordingly, the word quietly went out to friends and relatives. However, her scheme began to unravel when she entrusted Titus to deliver a note of invitation to his cousin Olive Louise in Lower Kingsburg – she of the doll's house, Raggedy Ann doll, and cut-out paper boats.

Titus became suspicious of the dispatch he was carrying. Why was it sealed? No recipe could be that secret. Anyway, recipes and such-like women's matters were never meant to be hidden in sealed envelopes. It didn't seem right. So before passing the envelope over to Olive, he insisted that the contents be revealed to him. Reluctantly she did so, after which he suggested they ought to organize a surprise of their own.

That evening the *Belsnickles* arrived in goodly numbers at the Mossman household. In fact there seemed to be a great many more than usual. Some groups came and went, as good *Belsnickles* are expected to do. But others just sat round drinking, and eating up all the special goodies that Helen Viola had laboured so long to prepare for the surprise birthday party. Chief among them, of course, were the invited guests. But she didn't know that. And where was Titus anyway? He hadn't shown up for dinner, and without a phone there was no way of checking up on his whereabouts. My sister Carolyn recalls that Mother was fairly beside herself with anxiety. Yet there was Titus, together with his cousin Olive, each well hidden beneath the garish rig of a *Belsnickle*, comfortably seated with all the other *Belsnickles* in the kitchen. Eventually, their identities were unmasked, much to Helen Viola's relief, and the surprise birthday party was rightly deemed a great success.

24

Omega
August 19, 1974, Rose Bay

... in what eternal, unstirring paralysis, and deadly, hopeless trance, yet lies antique Adam who died sixty round centuries ago; how is it that we still refuse to be comforted for those who we nevertheless maintain are dwelling in unspeakable bliss; why all the living so strive to hush all the dead; wherefore but the rumor of a knocking in a tomb will terrify a whole city. All these things are not without their meanings.

– Spoken by Ishmael
in Moby Dick
by Herman Melville

Father retired ashore in the late 1960s, keeping house and doing odd jobs in the community while Mother gradually eased out of teaching. Ironically, his last "real job" was as foreman of a pick and shovel gang in charge of enlarging a drainage ditch from Kingsburg Pond to Kingsburg Bay. This feature is located adjacent to the Graveyard Rocks, a stone's throw north of *Der Strandfriedhof*, the beachfront pioneer cemetery in

Lower Kingsburg. The Progressive Conservatives were in power that year, and Titus, a staunch supporter, though well up in years, got the job. I never saw him happier. Most savvy of the workers was Randy Wentzell, the local gravedigger. He would be on hand graveside a few years later to close out the last chapter in the old soldier's life.

During his last years at home Titus spent many hours in his large, upholstered rocking chair beside the kitchen windows, gazing out to sea, across the rise and fall of the tides. Few if any of his comrades in the 85th Battalion were still alive. Truth be known, he outlived his time. He recalled the close kinship forged during those desperate days and nightmare moments on the battlefields of France and Flanders. For blooded soldiers, the links are irrevocably fixed. Their glory, such as it is, may be a lie, but they are immutable; unable to forget, they need scarcely close their eyes to see their fallen comrades. Titus could never forget his best friend Billy, nor could he blot from memory the many traumatic life and death situations faced during his two years on the Western Front. From sheer repetition, etched in his mind were the trauma of going over, the sounds and sights of the conflict, and his band's bloody mindset of mad animal anger, fighting and killing in No Man's Land to ensure their own survival. Such is the sacrifice, a dark repression, of answering the call to war.

Titus, like Sir Patrick Stewart's dad (also a sergeant major), was at war's end a stranger even to himself. Sir Patrick, a famous English actor and a champion against domestic violence, writes of his father that in civilian life, "He was an angry, unhappy and frustrated man who was not able to control his emotions or his hands. As a child I witnessed his repeated violence against my mother, and the terror and misery he caused was such that, if I felt I could have succeeded, I would have killed him. If my mother had attempted it, I would have held him down. For those who struggle to comprehend these feeling in a child, imagine living in an environment of emotional unpredictability, danger and humiliation week after week."

With respect, much in this description fits Titus. However, although on occasion his hand was raised, some moral weight inhibited any follow-through blow struck against my mother. In retrospect, and in brief, from my perspective we were all extremely fortunate to have survived Passchendaele and all the rest.

Following a stroke in 1970, and an increasing number of unmanageable intervals at home, the dark side edged closer to the tipping point. His tinkering out of season with the family's firearms – long standing to attention in a hallway corner just off the kitchen – amidst mutterings threatening suicide and worse, led Mother to obtain the doctor's certificate from Dr. Barss to have Titus exercise a veteran's right to reside at Camp Hill Hospital in Halifax.

Only two problems: Camp Hill Hospital and Titus at this time were in transition to different states. Camp Hill's future lay in a mission to ambitiously restructure from its original 1917 status as lodgement for casualties of the Great War. For Titus, rebuilding was not an option. Consequently, he was transferred to Cole Harbour Hospital, the former Halifax County Rehabilitation Centre, ostensibly specializing in mental care. Unfortunately, at this time the Centre was of rather dubious reputation, having strayed far from both its mandate and financial means. Closed in 2001, and since used as a set for the antics of the television show *The Trailer Park Boys*, it was demolished early in 2012.

Titus lived out his last days at Cole Harbour, lucid enough to recognize and welcome visiting family members. He wished us well. Weeks before his final stroke, longing to go over the top one last time, he made known his chief need: release from the endless torture of confinement. The old soldier wonders why he continues to live after so many comrades have been lost, and to what end, worn out and helpless, nursed by strangers. My sister Carolyn, a chemist, recalls his specific enquiry concerning a possible means to the end: "You're a chemist, you must know of somet'ing I can take so I can die peacefully. I should never have lived so long. I'm no good for anyt'ing anymore, and there's no escape from here."

Mercifully, his voyage to Omega occurred August 19, 1974, at age eighty. Almost fifty-six years to the day earlier, at Amiens, he had won the Military Medal for "conspicuous gallantry in action." He was the last surviving member of a family of eleven children.

In fitting tribute, early on a Monday afternoon in high summer, his mortal remains were laid to rest in Harbourview Cemetery, Rose Bay. Randy Wentzell, the gravedigger, did the essential preparatory work, and stood by quietly at a distance to pay respects to his former trenching boss. The tide was falling as Titus's spirit was officially "fired out" by a party of sober old soldiers, who earlier doubled as pallbearers, standing steadily now at graveside.

"Present arms!"

"Prepare to fire!"

"Fire!"

In the overcast, the volley was muffled, much like those which fired the old year out and the stormy New Year in, on the occasion of his birth back in January 1, 1894. The shots were dull, mute music by comparison with the sound, light, and fury of the tons of jagged screaming metal that somehow dodged Titus on the battlefields of the Western Front in 1917-1918. Ironically, the salute to the old soldier was delivered courtesy of six .303 Lee-Enfield rifles. For the record, they were fired by comrades Haliburton Mossman, Carl Wamboldt, Leon Myra, Paul Mosher, Grant Eisenhauer and John Veldhoven.

25

Post-mortem (2014)

> *… total war is only sleeping. All the major states are still organized for war, and all that is needed for the world to slide back into a nuclear confrontation is a twist of the kaleidoscope that shifts international relations into a new pattern.*
>
> – *War*
> *Gwynne Dyer*

For all of us, certain events, however trivial, stand out in our memories for ready recall of our fathers. I shall always remember Titus's classic tale of how he overcame a crisis at sea:

"There was the time on that trip we run into some pretty rough weather. It was late in the day an' the wind come up hard just as the dories were returnin'. I put a big stew together. There was o' course a couple o' dozen men. Two table gangs. A bad cross-sea was runnin', an' damn if the ship didn't get beam ends on to a couple o' big 'uns … took to roll'n' so bad that the pot tipped right o'er the railin' roun' the stove. All o'er the galley floor, you! Sloppin' back and forth wit' the roll. What was I to do? Well, I grabbed the shovel out o' the coal scuttle and shovelled the whole mess best I could back into the pot, coal dust an' all. The men was just comin' down the fo'c's'le ladder. But they was so beat they never noticed nothin' a-tall. Swore it was the best stew ever! An' I never told 'em anyt'ing different."

No war story that, yet typical of the sort of acts of necessity learned under war conditions. Titus functioned in the close confines of the ship's galley with much the same quick and efficient woof and warp that drove him to solve the do and/or die issues of the day at Rosiéres and Dury. Quite apart from the element of chance, in which all soldiers firmly believe, according to survivors like Will R. Bird and Erich Maria Remarque, a great deal of skill was required to survive at the Front. And they ought to know.

There's little doubt that Titus's spartan upbringing and sea-acquired discipline served as the best kind of basic training for the military. His was an early start in a hard and dangerous occupation, and it helped to mold him as ideal NCO material. I seriously doubt that he was born a so-called "natural soldier," deriving a good deal of satisfaction in the job, and killing if he had to, provided that it was morally justified within the soldier's terms of reference. More likely, as his nightmares and recorded actions suggest, he struggled like most men to resolve the conflict of pride of place and position with the wastage he observed, and was from time to time called upon to execute, under soul-destroying circumstances. As an NCO wounded out to Étaples, he would have been unlikely to join the mutineers, no matter how just their cause. Then, following Amiens, his courage and sense of discipline in the line of duty being established beyond question, he was among those summoned to attend the training course for sergeant majors held regularly at Corps School.

Few Canadian family histories lack a military figure. Although the Great War is a century behind us, for each of the 60,661 Canadians who died, as for all participants, there are stories of pain and sorrow which, taken together, amount to a sort of national PTSD. For Titus's ancestors, time out of mind, war was a familiar way of life. It was a large factor leading them up to their point-of-no-return mid-eighteenth century voyage to Nova Scotia. Some of those same wars followed them across the North Atlantic. What does this chronicle of "wars and rumors of wars" mean?

According to anthropologists, we are the last surviving species of our family of primates. This is probably no accident, for we are ruthlessly competitive with any species that challenges us for space and food. We seem to be programmed according to a template laid down in prehistory. Like chimpanzees, with whom we share over 98 percent of our genetic identity, time and distance are reduced to what is required for us to function and survive. Our self-appointed stamp as *Homo sapiens* (translating to "wise earthly being") scarcely contributes to a more profound perspective. We have no natural understanding of sub-microscopic or nanno-scale worlds. Nor of the opposite order of magnitude, the distance to the sun, or the number of alien galaxies out there, billions of light-years removed from our own. *Homo*'s construct is not such as functions at those scales; ours is a tightly constrained middle path.

Pre-eminent American biologist E.O. Wilson argues that warfare is built into our genes. From an evolutionary perspective, chimps remain predisposed to aggression, war to the death, even cannibalism. Groups (troops) of wild chimps have been filmed making war on neighbouring communities of their own kind. Impossible to suppress, many of those earliest instincts cling to us still. We can lay claim to few if any new ones and the old ones are desperately difficult to shake.

Armed with the instincts of apes, we arrive as newborns poorly equipped to deal with the competition. Old habits are hard to change. From birth we must learn everything in order to conform to prevailing social mores, public opinion and law. As Patrick O'Brian observes in *Testimonies*, "All this, law, religion and all, is not enough to beat the old Adam." In the early going, our natural impulses were honed on how best to evade a predator, and on perfecting stone-throwing techniques.

In this respect very little has changed, except for the scale of the competition and the devastation lodged in modern missiles. At the tribal level, a band mentality of right and wrong was based on what worked best for the survival and common good of the family. But fast forward to the present when social media enable increasingly larger groups of people to perceive vested interests in peaceful coexistence. This mutation from earlier and isolated band mentalities should hold out some hope for the human condition. Unfortunately, only great power politicians cast deciding votes at the drumbeats of a crisis heralding possible chaos. Margaret MacMillan in *The War that Ended the Peace* points to Europe prior to 1914 as an example of chaos theory. Whatever the truth of the matter, no one foretold the nature and scale of the pending disaster. There is no doubt, however, that hair trigger of chance in human affairs played a major role, as exemplified by the assassination of Archduke Ferdinand at the very brink of war.

War has been a trademark of civilization. Fostered by kinship and ritual, the practice began gradually at the tribal level, swelling at intervals into sometimes monstrous proportion. Once at war, history shows that no nation will accept defeat until it has used up all weapons at its disposal. In the current global political forum, force as an argument is countered effectively only by a greater force, while reasons for war, as in the Great War, can cause a conflict to expand far beyond the importance of initial arguments. Dark forces beyond our control may take over – nationalism, revolution, religious zeal – though in the last analysis everything comes down to politics. Just beyond the realm of living memory the experience and lessons of the Great War haunt us yet. Perhaps the greatest lesson of all, to quote Niall Ferguson in *The War of the World*, is "the way that the leaders of apparently civilized societies were able to unleash the most primitive murderous instincts of their fellow citizens."

The mores and values promoted by a nation's military are quite different from those experienced by civilians. The army life appeals to the "old Adam." Basic training and combat experience ensure that a soldier learns how to do the job. And it is a terrifying job that this person is asked to do, with every action opposing the instinct for self-preservation. To the individual, the cost is tremendous self-sacrifice. And the collateral damage affects us all.

Acknowledgements

To those many friends who helped me complete this project I wish to express my indebtedness. Kate Kennedy, Mary Mahon, Andrea Mossman and Philip Mossman provided constructive criticism of early drafts of the manuscript. My wife Marie, sons Kaspar and Alexander, and daughter Andrea contributed encouragement and technical expertise. Cousins Norman and Albert Mossman advised on family records, and Donna, Albert and Paul Mossman provided photographs. George and Carolyn generously shared their memories of our father Titus. My thanks to Dan Sweeney, Coordinator of the Printshop, Acadia University, for his careful work with old documents; to Ralph Getson, Curator of the Fisheries Museum of the Atlantic, Lunenburg; to Philip Hartling, Reference Archivist, Nova Scotia Archives and Records Management, Halifax, and to James MacDonald, Baddeck, and Bruce MacDonald, Guysborough, for facilitating access to archival information; to Don Job, of the Kentville Legion, and to Brian McNally, librarian, Mount Allison University, for helpful advice freely given; to Penny, Brogan, Alice, and Lisa at the Memorial Library, Wolfville, likewise Nick, Gareth, Ed and Sophia at the associated Public Internet Access Site, for courteous, competent service; to Karl Carvery, Warrant

Officer, Aldershot Military Camp, Nova Scotia, William Rawling, Department of National Defense, Ottawa, and John Harrison and Gary Melville at Citadel Hill War Museum, Halifax, for guidance on Canadian Army lore and practice; to Manfred Richter for diligent research on German folk songs; to Gabrielle Wills for her keen insights into the Great War; to James Archibald and Lawrence Mawhinny for their counsel on Presbyterian Church records. Special thanks to my publisher Lesley Choyce and to Pottersfield editors Julia Swan and Peggy Amirault for their superb supporting roles.

Canadians are warmly received when visiting Great War battlefields of the Western Front. While on tour in September 2012, information and assistance was kindly supplied by Dominiek Dendoorven at In Flanders Fields Museum Documentation Centre, Ieper, Belgium; Steve Douglas and Milena Kolorikova, British Grenadier Bookshop, Ieper; Pierre Delcroix, citizen, Mons, Belgium; Piet De Roose, overseer at Brouwerij Van Steenberge, Ghent, Belgium; Carolyn Huot, guide, Vimy; Philippe Cailette, sage, Cambrai; Daniel Capelle, historian, Valenciennes; Marcelline Moore, guide, Le Musée Somme, Albert. Marianne Steenbrugge, Curator at Musée Quentovic, Étaples-sur-Mer, supplied valuable advice on Étaples and the British Expeditionary Force base camp during the Great War.

Suggested Further Readings

There is a vast literature on the Great War. To better appreciate the backdrop to the tragedy, *The Guns of August* (Barbara Tuchman: 1962) is highly recommended. As follow-up, *The Canadian Expeditionary Force 1914-1919* (G.W.L. Nicholson: 1962) provides one of the most comprehensive accounts along with *History of the Great War* (Basil H. Liddell Hart: 1972). Concerning the role of the 85th Battalion, Nova Scotia Highlanders, on the Western Front from February 1, 1917, to war's end, the *War Diary* objectively presents a wealth of factual detail; *The Eighty-fifth in France and Flanders* provides excellent supplementary material (Joseph Hayes: 1920). For the most part these works spare the reader the gut-wrenching close-ups which so overwhelm the senses in creative historical narratives such as *Birdsong: A Novel of Love and War* (Sebastian Faulks), *Three Day Road* (Joseph Boyden) and *The Brother Keepers* (John E. MacNintch). Library and Archives Canada, Ottawa, supplied a condensed version of Titus's military record in the 85th. The Works Consulted includes all references to sources used and to works cited.

Works Consulted

Alexander, Caroline, 2010. "The Shock of War," *Smithsonian*, September.

Allison, William, and Fairly, John, 1978. *The Monocled Mutineer*, London, Quartet Books.

Bairnsfather, Bruce, 1916. *Fragments from France*, London, "The Bystander," Tallis House.

Barbusse, Henri, 2003. *Under Fire*, New York, Penguin Group. (Translated from 1916 French publication by Robin Buss).

Barss, Peter, 1978. *Images of Lunenburg County*, Toronto, McClelland & Stewart.

Beatty, David Pierce, 1988. *Memories of the Forgotten War: The World War I Diary of Pte. V.E. Goodwin*, Baie Verte, New Brunswick, Baie Verte Editions.

Bell, Winthrop, 1961. *The "Foreign Protestants" and the Settlement of Nova Scotia*, Toronto, University of Toronto Press.

Berton, Pierre, 1986. *Vimy*, Toronto, McClelland & Stewart.

Berton, Pierre, 2001. *Marching as to War*, Toronto, Doubleday Canada.

Bird, Will R., 1968. *Ghosts Have Warm Hands*, Ottawa, CEF Books.

Borden, Brigadier-General Allison H., 1916. *A Short History and Photographic Record of the Nova Scotia Overseas Highland Brigade C.E.F: Composed of the 85th Nova Scotia Highlanders, 185th Cape Breton Highlanders, 193rd Nova Scotia Highlanders, 219 Overseas Highlanders*, Halifax, The Mortimer Company Ltd.

Bostyn, Frank, and Van der Fraeden, Jan, 2007. *Passchendaele 1917: The Story of the Fallen & Tyne Cot Cemetery*, Longview, Texas, Pen and Co.

Boyden, Joseph, 2005. *Three Day Road*, Toronto, Viking Canada (Penguin Group).

Boyne, John, 2011. *The Absolutist*, Toronto, Doubleday Canada.

Brindle, Sapper Walter, 1919. *France & Flanders: Four Years Experience Told in Poem & Story*, Charleston, South Carolina, Bibliolife. Available online at https://archive.org/details/franceflandersfo00brinuoft

Brown, Malcolm, 1978. *Tommy Goes to War*, London, J.M. Dent & Sons Ltd.

Buchanan, Patrick J., 2008. *Churchill, Hitler, and the Unnecessary War*, New York, Crown Publishing Group (Random House Inc.).

Bull, Stephen, 2010. *Trench*, London, Osprey Publishing, in association with the Imperial War Museum.

Burg, David F., and Purcell, E.L., 1998. *Almanac of World War I*, Lexington, The University Press of Kentucky.

Churchill, Winston, 1931. *The World Crisis, 1911-1918*. London, Penguin Books.

Clark, Christopher, 2012. *The Sleepwalkers: How Europe Went to War in 1914*, New York, Harper Collins.

Clements, Captain Robert N., 2013. *Merry Hell: The Story of the 25th Battalion (Nova Scotia Regiment), Canadian Expeditionary Force 1914-1919*, Ed. Brian Douglas Tennyson, Toronto, University of Toronto Press.

Clint, Mabel B., 1934. *Our Bit: Memories of War Service by a Canadian Nursing Sister*, Montreal, R.V.H. Alumnae Association.

Cook, Tim, 2007. *At the Sharp End: Canadians Fighting the Great War 1914-1916*, v. 1, Toronto, Viking Canada (Penguin Group).

Cook, Tim, 2008. *Shock Troops: Canadians Fighting the Great War 1917-1918*, v. 2, Toronto, Viking Canada (Penguin Group).

Creighton, Helen, 1976. *Folklore of Lunenburg County, Nova Scotia*, Toronto, McGraw-Hill Ryerson Ltd.

Cross, Tim, 1988. *The Lost Voices of World War I*, London, Bloomsbury.

Davis, Wade, 2012. *Into the Silence: the Great War, Mallory, and the Conquest of Everest*, Toronto, Knopf Canada.

DesBrisay, Mather Byles, 1967. *History of the County of Lunenburg*, Third Edition. Bridgewater, The Bridgewater Bulletin Ltd.

Dyer, Gwynne, 1985. *War*, New York, Stoddart.

Dyer, Gwynne, 2004. *War* (The New Edition), Toronto, Random House Canada.

Englund, Peter, 2011. *The Beauty and the Sorrow*, New York, A.A. Knopf. (Translated from the Swedish by Peter Graves).

Evans, Susan, and Crankshaw, Jean, 2011. *Canadians at War*, Fredericton, New Brunswick, Goose Lane Editions.

Faulks, Sebastian, 1988. *Birdsong: A Novel of Love and War*, New York, Vintage Press.

Ferguson, Niall, C. D., 1998. *The Pity of War*, New York, Basic Books (a member of the Perseus Books Group).

Ferguson, Niall, C.D., 2006. *The War of the World*, New York, Penguin Press.

Fischer, H.C., and Dubois, E.X., 1937. *Sexual Life During the Great War*, London, Francis Aldor Publisher.

Follett, Ken, 2010. *Fall of Giants*, London, Dutton (Penguin Group).

Fox, Brent, 1983. *Camp Aldershot: serving since 1904*, Kentville, Nova Scotia, The Kings Historical Society.

Francis, Diana, 2004. *Rethinking War and Peace*, London, Pluto Press.

Freeman, Bill, and Nielson, Richard, 1999. *Far From Home*, Toronto, McGraw-Hill Ryerson.

Graham, Bruce, 2013. *Duddy Doesn't Live Here Anymore*, Lawrencetown Beach, Nova Scotia, Pottersfield Press.

Graves, Robert, 1929. *Goodbye to All That*, London, Cassell.

Gray, David R., 2002. "Carrying Canadian Troops: The Story of R.M.S. Olympic as a First World War Troopship," *Canadian Military History* Vol. 11 #1.

Grossman, Dave, 1995. *On Killing*, Boston, Little, Brown and Company.

Hadley, Michael L., 1985. *U-boats Against Canada*, Montreal, McGill-Queen's Press.

Hardy, Thomas, 1898. *Wessex Poems*, New York, Harper and Brothers.

Harrison, Mark, 2010. *The Medical War: British Military Medicine in the First World War*, London, Oxford University Press.

Hastings, Max, 2013. *Catastrophe: Europe Goes to War 1914*, New York, Alfred A. Knopf.

Hayes, Geoffrey, Iarocci, Andrew, and Bechthold, Mike, 2007. *Vimy Ridge – a Canadian Reassessment*, Waterloo, Ontario, Wilfred Laurier University Press.

Hayes, Joseph, 1920. *The Eighty-fifth in France and Flanders*, Halifax, Nova Scotia, Royal Print and Litho Ltd. Available online at https://archive.org/details/eightyfifthinfra00hayeuoft

Helprin, Mark, 1991. *A Soldier of the Great War*, New York, Harcourt Brace Jovanovich.

Herwig, H. Holger, 2009, *The Marne, 1914: The Opening of World War I and the Battle that Changed the World*, New York, Random House.

Hibberd, Dominic, 2002. *Wilfred Owen: A New Biography*, London, Phoenix.

Hierschfeld, M., 1930. *Sitter Geschichte des Weltkriegs Erster Band*. Wien, Verlag für Sexualwissenschaft. Schneider & Co.

Hitler, Adolf., 1927. *Mein Kampf*, New York, Mariner Books (Houghton Mifflin Co.) (Translated from the German by Ralph Manheim).

Hunt, M. Stuart, 1920. *Nova Scotia's Part in the Great War*, Halifax, Nova Scotia, The Nova Scotia Veteran Publishing Co. Limited. Available online at https://archive.org/details/novascotia00huntuoft

Hyatt, A.M.J., 1987. *General Sir Arthur Currie: A Military Biography*, University of Toronto Press.

Jessop, Violet, 2004. *Titanic Survivor: The Newly Discovered Memoirs of Violet Jessop Who Survived Both the Titantic and Britannic Disasters*, Introduced and edited by John Maxtone-Graham, Dobbs Ferry, New York, Sheridan House.

Kaye, M.M., 1996. *Rudyard Kipling: The Complete Verse*, London, Kyle Cathie Ltd.

Keller, Richard, 2009. *The German Soldier in World War I*, http://www.greatwar.com/scripts/openExtra.asp?extra=10 (Date accessed January 7, 2013)

Knight, Edward Frederick, 1920. *The Union Castle and the War*, London, The Union Castle Mail Steamship Co. Ltd.

Lewis, C. Day, ed. 1963. *The Collected Poems of Wilfred Owen*, New York, A New Direction Book.

Liddell Hart, Basil H., 1930. *History of the First World War*, London, Cassell and Co. Ltd.

Lotz, Jim, 1990. *Canadians at War*, London, Bison Books Ltd.

MacDonald, W. James, 2007. *Honour Role of the Nova Scotia Overseas Highland Brigade 85th, 185th, 193rd, 219th Battalions*, Sydney, Cape Breton University Press.

MacLennan, Hugh, 1941. *Barometer Rising*, Toronto, McClelland & Stewart Ltd.

MacMillan, Margaret, 2001. *Paris, 1919*, New York, Random House.

MacMillan, Margaret, 2013. *The War that Ended the Peace*, Toronto, Profile.

MacNintch, John E. (Ted), 2007. *The Brother Keepers*, Old Saybrook, CT., AquaDoc Publications.

MacPhail, Andrew, 1925. *Official History of the Canadian Forces in the Great War 1914-19: The Medical Services*, Ottawa, King's Printer. Available online at http://www.cmp-cpm.forces.gc.ca/dhh-dhp/his/docs/CFGW_MedSvc_e.pdf and https://archive.org/details/medicalservices00macpuoft

Major, Kevin, 1995. *No Man's Land*, Toronto, Doubleday Canada Ltd.

Manchester, William, 1964. *The Arms of Krupp*, London, Little, Brown & Co.

Mann, Susan, 2005. *Margaret MacDonald: Imperial Daughter*, Montreal, McGill-Queen's University Press.

Marsden, Lorna, R., 2012. *Canadian Women and the Struggle for Equality*, Oxford University Press.

McMeekin, Sean, 2013. *July 1914: Countdown to War*, Toronto, Ikon.

Melville, Herman, 1956. *Moby Dick*, (Edited by Alfred Kazin), Boston, Houghton Mifflin Co.

Morris, Desmond, 1967. *The Naked Ape*, New York, Dell Publishing, Random House.

Mossman, Philip, L., 2000. *In Search of David* (self-published).

Nicholson, Col. Gerald W.L., 1962. *Canadian Expeditionary Force 1914-1919: The Official History of the Canadian Army in the First World War*, Ottawa, Queens Printer and Controller of Stationery. Available online at http://www.cmp-cpm.forces.gc.ca/dhh-dhp/his/docs/CEF_e.pdf

O'Brian, Patrick, 1952. *Testimonies*, New York, W.W. Norton and Co.

Oldham, Peter, 1997. *Battleground Europe*, Barnsley, U.K., Pen and Sword Books Ltd.

Remarque, Erich Maria, 1928. *All Quiet on the Western Front*, New York, Fawcett Crest. (Translated from the German by A.W. Wheen).

Richter, Manfred, 1883. "The Custom of 'Shooting in' and 'Wishing in' the New Year in Lunenburg County, Nova Scotia," *Deutschkanadische Studien, Annals* v. 4, p. 97-106.

Riggs, Bert, ed. 2007. *Grand Bank Soldier: The War Letters of Lance Corporal Curtis Forsey*, St John's, Newfoundland, Flanker Press.

Ripley, Donald, F., 1991. *The Homefront: Wartime Life in Camp Aldershot and Kentville, Nova Scotia*. Hantsport, Nova Scotia, Lancelot Press.

Robertshaw, Andrew, and Kenyon, David, 2008. *Digging the Trenches: The Archaeology of the Western Front*, Barnsley, U.K., Pen and Sword Books Ltd.

Roze, Anne, 2000. *Fields of Memory*, London, Cassell.

Ruck, Calvin, W., 1987. *The Black Battalion 1916-1920: Canada's best kept military secret*, Halifax, Nova Scotia, Nimbus Publishing Ltd.

Sassoon, Siegfried, 1961. *Collected Poems: 1908-1956*, London, Faber and Faber.

Sheldon, Jack, 2009. *The German Army at Cambrai*, Barnsley, U.K., Pen and Sword Books Ltd.

Sheldon, Jack, 2012. *The German Army on the Western Front 1915*, Barnsley, UK., Pen and Sword Books Ltd.

Sheldon, Jack. *The German Army at Vimy Ridge 1914-1917*, Barnsley, UK., Pen and Sword Books Ltd.

Stewart, Patrick, 2009. "The Legacy of Domestic Violence," *The Guardian*, November 27, p. 4.

Strachan, Hew, 2004. *The First World War*, New York, Viking Penguin.

Swettenham, John, 1968. *MacNaughton*, v. 1, (1887-1939). Toronto, Ryerson Press.

Thomas, Louisa, 2011. *Conscience*, New York, Penguin Press.

Travers, Tim, 1992. *How the War was Won*, London, Routledge.

Tuchman, Barbara, 1962. *The Guns of August*, New York, MacMillan Company.

Turner, John, ed. 1987. *Britain and the First World War*, Boston, Unwin Hyman.

War Diary – Nova Scotia Highlanders 12 Infantry Brigade – 4th Canadian Division, (Transcribed by Edward Tainton). Available online at http://cefresearch.ca/matrix/War%20 Diaries/transcribed/bn085/bn085y1917-1919.pdf

Whiston, William (trans.), 1757. *The Complete Works of Josephus Flavius*, London, T. Nelson and Sons.

Whitehead, Ian R., 1988. *Doctors in the Great War*, Barnsley, U.K., Leo Cooper.